SIGNIFICANT OTHERS

Left Luggage Poetry

MARK BARRY

ALSO by MARK BARRY

POETRY
THE TRUTH TAILORED TO SUIT
(Shoulder Length Poems about the End of the World and Other Worries)

MY BROKEN HEART
(75 Days In The NHS)

FILM
KEEPERS and SLEEPERS
Movies You Probably Haven' Seen Plus Some You Should Own
And The Best Formats To Get em On

SCREENPLAYS
THE CLOTHS OF HEAVEN
(The 1990s Northern Ireland Peace Process)

AN ENGLISH LADY
(Life Story of Eglantyne Louisa Jebb, Founder of Save The Children)

SILAS
(Irish Politician's Journey Back from the Loss of a Son)

FULL OF GRACE
(Love Story around 9/11 atrocities as a way of National Healing)

INTERNET REFERENCES
AMAZON UK
Over 4,180 Reviews on a Wide Range of Subjects
Hall of Fame Reviewer Six Times

AMAZON AUTHOR'S PAGE
Type the following into any Search Engine - B00LQKMC6I

SOUNDS GOOD, LOOKS GOOD Blogger Site
Over One Million Six-Hundred Thousand Views

Copy the following into any Search Engine
https://markattheflicks.blogspot.com/

ALSO BY MARK BARRY

The *Sounds Good Music Books* Series (30 Titles)
All-Genre Guides to Exceptional CD Reissues and Remasters
Available on all AMAZON Sites as Downloadable e-Books

YEAR Volumes
VOODOO CHILE – 1968
WHOLE LOTTA LOVE – 1969
ALL THINGS MUST PASS – 1970
GET IT ON – 1971
TUMBLING DICE – 1972
US AND THEM – 1973
PICK UP THE PIECES – 1974
CAPT. FANTASTIC – 1975
MORE THAN A FEELING – 1976
PROVE IT ALL NIGHT – 1977 to 1979

DECADE Volumes
GIMME SHELTER! - Classic 1960s Rock & Pop
ALL RIGHT NOW – Classic Rock & Pop 1970 – 1974 – A to L
REASON TO BELIEVE – Classic Rock & Pop 1970 to 1974 – M to Z

GENRE Volumes
CADENCE / CASCADE – Prog, Psych, Avant Garde (1966 to 1976)
SOUL GALORE! – 60ts Soul, 60ts R&B, Northern, Mod, New Breed,
Rare Groove
HIGHER GROUND – 70ts Soul, Funk and Jazz Fusion
BOTH SIDES NOW – 1960s and 1970s Folk & Country Music & Rock
Thereabouts
MANNISH BOY – Blues, Rhythm 'n' Blues, Vocal Groups, Doo Wop &
Rockabilly

THEMED Volumes
I SAW THE LIGHT – Overlooked Albums 1955 to 1979 (480-plus titles)
LOOKING AFTER NO. 1 – Debut Albums 1956 to 1986 Vol. 1 – A to L
LOOKING AFTER NO. 1 – Debut Albums 1956 to 1986 Vol. 2 – M to Z
URGE TO SPLURGE – The First Ten Years Of Double-Albums 1966 to 1976
SOMETHING'S HAPPENING HERE Volumes 1 to 7 – 1960's & 1970s (7 Books)
LET'S GO CRAZY – 1980s Music on CD – Exceptional CD Remasters
GOODY TWO SHOES – 2CD Deluxe Editions and Compilations 50s to 00s

4

CONTENTS

6

CONTENTS cont'd...

CONTENTS cont'd...

CONTENTS cont'd...

CONTENTS cont'd...

CONTENTS cont'd...

CONTENTS cont'd...

CONTENTS cont'd...

13

CONTENTS cont'd...

For all the SIGNIFICANT OTHERS in my life
Too numerous to mention, too broke to pay...

Love and Lubricants
MARK

Cover Photo:
Handmade Baby Shoes for Our First Born, Dean, Aged 1

MEMOS FROM THE BURNING BUSH

There are three beautiful sounds in life

The sound of children playing in a schoolyard
The sound of women laughing
The sound of finding your own voice...

BALUSTRADES and PENCILS

Approximating functionality
Our new *old* home is a strange combination
Of rickety paint-shaved balustrades and perfectly paired pencils
Stood erect like a badly congealed Punk Rock hair-do
In a Property of the Boss mug (on my desk) missing its handle...

My honeycombed corniced high-ceiling rear-aspect bedroom
Doubles up as a Man Cave for shelved CDs and Hardbacks Books
Most of which never get touched or used
And should be on eBay making us some filthy lucre

But ours is not to question or philosophize on renovational fervour
On the deeper meaning of stair components
Or nicely symmetrical clumps of eraser-headed graphite dispensers
In a china clay receptacle I should have binned years ago

Ours is to repair and maintain and caulk such castle/kingdom anomalies
Regardless of their fiscal pit-of-peril bank-account buggering
As we bravely poo-poo the effects of leaky loo scullery invasions
And wave at gossamer seagulls that just shat on a small
Nuclear Submarine with its missile-doors open
On a training exercise off the coast of Margate...

Ours is to know that one-day
Wafting ethereal across another plane of Nirvanic existence

We shall titter, all-knowingly, at such previous corporeal irritants
Flying in the face of obvious builder's bollox
(Just fix the fucking thing mate for the price you quoted
And the promises you made)

As we smirk, like British MPs do
When asked a direct question
Someone in the public
Expects an actual answer to...

I LIKE THAT

I like your funky ankle-high petal-patterned Doc Martens
People enquire on the street; they burst into a grin
See you bring the season's first daffodils down to Angela
A fellow gardener and friend; cuppa, natter within

I love how you use Margate Mercury newspaper cut outs
To make a glued lampshade for a cog-wheel stem
Tininess of your sock-couplets in a canvas laundry basket
Huge-paged curvaceous art pieces, I also like them

How you TV cringed when Roe vs. Wade got overturned
Shrinkwrap a dinner for your incapacitated mother
Letting the cat sleep on your side of the Leonardo duvet
Who gulp-eyes me like I'm Villanelle's scarier brother

And when you do silly voices with the kids on the mobile
Sharing a laugh, latest goss, biggest celebrity twat
I like the fact that our house and street is better for you
Being in it, here, complimenting all of us. I like that...

For MARY ANN

ASPIRATIONAL MIDGE and MADGE
(Bully Boy Stain)

With the best will in the world and charitable poise
It's hard to rid yourself of a certain thought
The world is full of cunts, insufferable indoctrinated
And your reasoning will amount to naught

You learn harsh lessons in life about the tormentors
The smiling-beguiling with cutesy bushy tails
They'll saw ladder steps from beneath your ascent
Offer comfort, as they future-index your fails

Theirs is the perpetual undercut; crave to demean
Impart their negativity like parasitic disease
You spend a lifetime in relationships and shitty jobs
Countering their jabs, navigating appease

Sometimes you can harness tough, just overcome
But on other occasions, you limp-foot away
Precariously balancing on a life navigational rung
Where you chose flight over embattled stay

Aspirational Midge and Madge go social climbing
They probably have a healthy crush on gain
But it's *bully mentality* you need to really cauterize
Suture that wound daily; wipe away its *stain*...

ORANGE-TIP WHITES, RED ADMIRALS and LASCARS

In our walled secret garden outback, White Butterflies bolt
Red Admirals flutter over the elevated flowery front
Our respective gals attack dual choreographed greenery
They've been at it five years, always eager to punt

Angela diligently prunes and tends to her roadside display
Chicken-wiring old railings to keep new foxes out
Mary Ann de-stones hard soil and plant-arranges the beds
Pours life-giving water, countering frazzle drought

I have no aptitude for gardening like my brother Jonathan
My sister Catherine in Dublin, gifted with the same
I type away like a Shakespeare and Spike Milligan combo
Window admire their knack, how-to-chaos tame

The Orange-Tip Whites are pretty as they pollinate flowers
But the Red Admirals are spectacular, casual alight
They mate in swirling pairs, dancing up into the heat drifts
Then settle on your walls and hands, a stunning sight

We left the city to get away from pollution/over-crowding
Get back to nature, walk old fields, dip into the sea
Wander beaches with froth and spume like Lascar Sailors
Catmint our lives with new beginners for you, for me

But as I watch our ladies battle for what must be nurtured
Kneading their love into soil, spinning blossom plates
I know why God made the female our Constant Gardiner
Allotment Angels, Queen Bees, Keeper of the Gates

They are the vessels of living, underwriters of continuance
Flitting butterflies from one pollen portal to another
So I look with awe at nature's outlaws, unclipping holsters
Should some slug try his luck with any earth mother...

For MARY ANN, ANGELA, CATHERINE and JONATHAN
Pals of Nature

TIME FOR BULLS

These days I don't swing from chandeliers in a lurid Mankini
And she don't bother neighbours with orgasmic cries
In fact, according to some, we're not sexy people anymore
Old and in the way, best embrace our wrinkled eyes

So nowadays, it's all sensible shoes and wraparound slippers
Busy counting out heart tablets, prophylactics binned
Whilst millennials look at us as rosewatered geriatric swingers
Is only their generation that humped fucked & sinned

So, as the pee dribble and uncontrollable farts come thither
And we laugh at sag, muscle ache and balding skulls
We wonder will youngsters boast so cocksure in their dotage
When *time* is more precious than any strutting of bulls...

FLOSSING WITH THE LORD OF ALL CREATION

As God Almighty, I fret incessantly over all of my fabulous creations
Heaving cleavage, perforated teabags and Terry Towels
I'm in floods at carpet, electrical circuitry and Webster dictionaries
Racked and stacked with sexpot consonants and vowels

I get my sustainably sourced cotton knickers in one non-binary knot
At my vast array of paintbrushes, linseed oils and cement
I practically masturbate myself flaccid at footage of dolphin shoals
My ethereally glowing love phallus all out of shape, bent

There was one day in July 2020 there, when I descended to Blighty
Met with that insufferable smartarse Mark Barry for a brew
But fuck me sideways in my Godlike rectum, but the man can talk
He's worse than the boy going on about his Judean crew

Of course what I can't let them know as an all-knowing Godhead
Is that despite an IQ of a zillion, I'm still learning on the job
If I reveal my inadequacies to the huddled masses and proletariat
They'll say I'm a stupid cunt, or worse, an upper class snob

So I sit up here daydreaming about Banksy' identity and silk worms
The length of rivers, giraffe legs, smell of a newborn's skin
I flick through albums of world's forming, lava flows and eruptions
Flossing keenly as I forgive *both* original *and* unoriginal sin

But of all my better moments versus my questionable experiments
I admit a raging boner for Planet Earth's myriad Humanity
So excuse me while I try to finalize this frigging Expanding Universe
And regarding a better Eden, *pray* for a workaholic deity...

UNEXPECTED RAYS

It's cloudy today on platter No. 13 of our July 2021 summer holidays
Daily rituals and routines established, keeping up schedules
Our severely Autistic son Dean hand flapping out in the turbulence
A grown man of 30, gangly and milky and visibly childlike
My better half Mary Ann braving the ebbing tides of Westgate Beach
As the cold ripple-waves body slap and sharp inhale both of them...

Yesterday, a WWII Spitfire flew low over these virtually people-less sands
Its combat-veteran Merlin Engine roaring, distinctive elliptical wingspan
Cutting through the invisible ambivalence, Rolls Royce icon of the skies
There are said to be only three working versions left in the Thanet area
Regularly transporting paying customers along the white cliffs of Dover
A literal embodiment of courage and triumph of spirit over adversity

I watch Mary Ann float, scope Dean's moves in his belly-high trunks
Guarding against murderous mud sinkholes between red/yellow flags

There's gobby youths playing their wireless micro boom-boxes too loud
Crappy discordant dance music regardless of the cost to the sensitive

As I sit on the concrete promenade with our blue IKEA bag of towelling
I'm singing an effecting Randy Newman song - *Every Time It Rains*
I can't get it out of my head. And like all true emotional practitioners
Toy Story-beloved Randy has penned a tune that nails, rams, corners us
Up against life's gym-wall, playing punch-bag with your slippery heart...

Lathered with Factor-50 on his white-as-snow torso, both arms in the air
Our Dino yelps and auti-blurts, like those army ordinance sonic booms
That thunder triumphant from miles away across this open expanse

In the French coast distance, black storm cloud streaks are snarling
And overcome with decades of unbearable sadness, I can't help it
I shed a hurt tear none of those chorus-obsessed yobbos will notice

But just as the melancholy threatens to kick up in into another gear
I watch as gorgeous unexpected rays suddenly bathe my loved ones
Shafting down from the sky onto my soldier duo
Elliptical in their Merlin engine stance
Dealing with the next wave of unrelenting slaps and mind pounds
Loins girded, facing down those torpedoes that must be damned...

ILL-GOTTEN GAINS

It's hard to root out a deeply programmed deception
The safety first of an embattled head
We're supposed to embrace onward personal growth
But switch on sabotage-mode instead

Far too easy to indulge in this artful backwards contest
Same old song on someone else's stage
Endlessly rewinding putz thinking on paper and couch
For earnest upstarts, half my fucking age

You look for legacy as the dotage decades approach
Balls lick an old dog overqualified for zip
It's humiliating to find yourself another deep dive gaslit
Mr. Past It atop his emotional rubbish tip

So I bench any worry about other people's judgement
And pursue individuality as the only road
I beg, borrow, rob and steal to become my proper self
No longer bear their jealous gobby goad

It's hard to root out comfortable embedded behaviour
Slavishly losing out to fear's bloody stains
But I must train my brain to be a personal Robber Baron
Thieve back 'me' and such ill-gotten gains...

AMBASSADOR TRIPLE BILL

The domed old-school Ambassador Cinema in O'Connell Street
Used to be the fleapit of choice for cheap daytime flicks
They'd cram the Balcony Area with budget-conscious Sci-Fi nuts
Carrying a *Lord Of The Rings* paperback the size of bricks

So we took our premium seats with Smarties Tube and Popcorn
Guzzling a Jumbo Coke for the *Star Wars Triple Marathon*
Me with my brother Damien hoovering the original Lucas trilogy
Six hours of Skywalker and Vadar and the Jedi Obi-Wan

Those opening battleship sequences blew our tiny Dublin minds
Ludicrously creative and edge-of-your seat visual shots
We'd drool at Princess Leia in a skimpy outfit, galactic negligee
While chomping on a Curly Wurly chased by Jelly Tots

The loo became a pressing need half way through The Empire
But it risked your missing Lando Calrissian striking back
So you'd rush out during the miniscule interval curtain closures
Return to see the Millennium Falcon Death Star attack

How did we manage such enthusiasm and energy outpouring?
And why does it still exert such an intensely special pull
Because we were family, doing what we loved to do together
Sat there in that fantasy, immersed, rapt, our hearts full...

For my brother DAMIEN

BICYCLE CLIPS

Just relieved of another bottle of wine from underneath his filthy coat
There's an alchie rugby scrumming back from the exit doors in Aldi's
Screaming bile-threats and faux-protests with his even filthier mouth
Being unceremoniously chucked out by three sick-of-it burly bouncers

There's a 20-something homeless lad outside the Post Office One-Stop
His sheepish mongrel lying on an outspread army camouflage coat
A flayed cap in front of his makeshift blanket inviting kind passers-by
To add breakfast to his sprinkled coins and my lucky-dip lottery ticket

Opposite Central Pharmacy with its permanently-on security cameras
Is a ruddy-faced woman and her strip of super strength *Special Brew*
Sat by two older leery men, all clutching and supping and pretending
To be having a right laugh with mates on a February Saturday morning

Her haunted look reeks of years of being passed around social services
Way too young to be benched beneath St. Paul's broken clock tower
Strangulating a gold and black lettered tin, luxury branded, seductive
The merciless bone-cold sea wind whipping up nearby Edgar Road

In the Old Town, I spot a tight-spokes gent outside the Pilgrim's Hospice
Looking flax dapper and impossibly fit for his seriously advanced years
Probably heard the doodlebugs scream/cut out when he was a nipper
His latest hardback acquisition stretch-strapped to his jutting rear rack

We connect for a moment as our eyes meet, glancing down at what
Some might ridicule as fuddy-duddy, embarrassingly naff and passé
Bicycle clips, tucking in his britches, stemming the unrelenting dirt-creep

And armed with the right equipment, he pushes off, all spry and calm
His oil-protecting clip-ons facing the seafront blast as if it wasn't there
Off home to luxuriate in his latest passed-on knowledge enhancing find
Simple things keeping him safe and clean
Family, education, regimen, code

And perhaps unawares of his fate in subtle decisions and good choices
Journey protectorate given to him by loving others
A long, long, *lucky* time ago...

PLAYING PATIENCE WITH THE BEATLES

To start my creative day, I play 'Patience With The Beatles'
Fifty-three card illustrations in the official Apple pack
And if I get out five descending sets of alternating colours
I'll hammer productivity on my ancient upstairs Mac

This ritualistic nonsense probably wouldn't pass any critique
As the Ace Of Spades turns over on 1970's *Let It Be*
But I love seeing *Revolver* show up on the King of Diamonds
Four of Hearts, live on the *Ed Sullivan Show*, US TV

King of Clubs has them walking across *Abbey Road* in 1969
With cryptic Volkswagen Beetle and a shoeless Paul
Queen Of Diamonds depicts a cherubic *Please Please Me*
Seven of Hearts *Magical Mystery Tour*, bus madrigal

Five of Spades has them wearing snow capes filming *Help!*
Ace of Diamonds, portraits from the *Double White*
Nine of Hearts has a bearded John walking Tittenhurst Park
About to spring a *Revolution* on *Hey Jude* tonight

The Queen of Clubs shows their mop-top haircuts circa '63
Seven of Diamonds has *Sgt. Peppers* Fixing A Hole
But of all the cards, I like the transition ones after *Yesterday*
Where they morphed into artists with *Rubber Soul*

I bought and sold their LPs and 45-Singles as part of my job
Twenty years filtering out their stunning catalogue
Greatness leaves a legacy that echoes across generations
The rest of us chasing the creative hair of the dog

Will we ever see their like again; know such musical genius?
When every release thrilled and properly amazed?
I don't know. But I'm a *Paperback Writer;* I'm working it out
Honing it, daily inspired by the artistry they blazed...

For JOHN, PAUL, GEORGE and RINGO
And their astonishing legacy of joy

AGE-OLD WEAVE

Mary Ann is Feng coordinating curtains with our downstairs neighbours
Four drapes of oyster-coloured Shantung silk, eighteen spun meters
Cotton-lined by Angela across days of heroic sewing and weaving
Bob fearlessly atop an unfeasibly high ladder's squeaky stand-plate
Pelmet hooking these flash-looking satin sheers with puddle hems...

They're classy, like the sixteen-foot windows of our ancient home
Somehow right in this year-and-a-half of misery and closed shops
Beautiful in the face of so much loss, a proper plum drop to those
Horrible high numbers we saw on TV, month after haunting month

It's been a simple domestic pleasure, helping each other out like this
Lifting up the old brownstone gal and her flaking front window display
Looking a little worse for wear after 125-years of icky bodge-it-and-go
Sea-smashing sonic-boom wind and squawking poop-psycho gulls

There's satisfaction in working for a result, building something up with
Our endlessly practical cohabiters who have since become good pals
Until the fruits of our labours bear out that age-old weave of wisdom
A problem halved is a problem solved...coming out of lockdown...

I'm reminded of Aileen in No. 6 taking months to regen her garden
With potted plants and painted paving stones, accepting shrubs
And wee Ruby Rose next door in No. 3 Clarendon Road
An all-dancing Munchkin waving from her huge first-floor windowpanes
Giddy at the sight of neighbours she knows, smiling back affectionately
Eager to show off her newest fantastical Dad-given dolly acquisition
That's only fully good if the whole world sees her joy

Peeking out from behind those playful drapes
At a street full of possibilities
At adults moving about once again

At faces lifted up
Surrendering anew
To the old school nurture of a proper share...

For our neighbours BOB & ANGELA in 4A, AILEEN in 6, RUBY ROSE in 3

LIMPETS ON THE ROCKS

We've a framed photograph over our stand-alone bath
On the first landing area of our 19th century home
Shot by renowned early pioneer Frank Meadow Sutcliffe
Circa 1876 to 1880, black and white, Whitby foam

It shows two ragged sisters, late teens, smiling at camera
Probably astonished at the new fangled apparatus
A chronicler of working lives in his beloved fishing village
His North Yorkshire shots reeked of caring, not status

The bearded Sutcliffe had won 60-plus portraiture medals
Was bestowed an Honorary Fellowship by his peers
His often harsh and unflinchingly honest black and whites
Regularly reproduced for posterity across the years

The giddy subjects were on an east-cliff bedrock beach
Called *The Scaur*, callous hands from *flither-picking*
A *Flither* is a limpet/mollusc that fishermen used for bate
Provided them an income; winter comes a-kicking

Their expressions are ones of hope, fun and youthfulness
A world of possibilities I'm sure he wanted to frame
They may have been dirt poor, down the pecking order
But they had dreams like us, longings just the same

And I often wonder in passing as I clock their expressions
Did they beat grinding poverty; maybe even thrive
Were they blessed with children of their own, all prosper
Regaling that moment over hearths, thankful, alive

He doesn't name the gregarious sisters, futures so fated
As they limpet on rocks, a century and a half ago
But I often think of them and all those forgotten people
Remembered by a big heart, catching life in flow...

DICK/NON-DICK RATIO

I'm reading about some moralising toerag woke fuckturd
Who's ranting on about gender and binary code
I can't make head or tail of their self-righteous arguments
As they drop yet another hip-hateful online load

I identify as a non-binary transgender no testicles coconut
Or is it a clitoral melon in recycled vegan overalls
There has to be a point when someone calls time on labels
And kicks such political correctness in its tiny balls

How does any of this bile advance our collective learning?
When it's just another version of an eye for an eye
So forgive me if I offend your delicate right-on sensibilities
But please fuck right off you dick/non-dick, and die...

FACING THE SWELL
(Another Time)

Antony Gormley's in-situ bronze statue *Another Time* faces out to sea
His arse pert to the Margate weather and the Turner Museum behind
Mary Ann and I photograph his form on the low tide with our iPhones
Our son Dean giggling, the motionless sculpture in shot behind his cap

The full tide swallows the strangely moving art installation twice a day
And his survival-revelation when the engulfing recedes never fails to stir
Like a sailor safely home from a voyage, his battered limbs on dry land
Hugging loved ones once more who had stood on the shore distraught

Months later Dean is home again from his Special Needs Community
And out of the blue in the back seat of our car, it happens in an instant
A full-on Epileptic Fit that grips his entire body in seizure, hands gnarled
Moaning and twisting, choking for air, eyes rolling back, 27 years old...

We've been told its late-onset-epilepsy, common in people with Autism
But nothing prepares you for the terror and the helplessness when it hits
MA pulled over by the side of the road phoning 999 in tears and panic
As Daddy holds his boy and tries to keep him safe as he writhes...

Weeks later, I can't get the rapid-response paramedic out of my mind
Quietly sat in our living room, the machinery of saving all around him
The reality of pressure pads and finger gauges and duplicate form-fills

Working steadily, with patience, dedication, smart probing questions
Keeping calm, keeping a watchful distance, allowing re-orientation
Dean throwing up into a glass as the racking turned his insides out
Flopped on my shoulder exhausted, confused, an adult-man childlike...

I look out on the famous Margate sunset and its gorgeous riot of colours
The sea having slowly receded, allowing the sands to dry and breathe
Safe now, Dean is home with no reoccurrence but an MRI on the way...

And I watch the relentlessness of the tide turning - it will be back soon
Possibly even stronger and more engulfing-violent than the last assault
Thrashing at our collective work of art, who just troops through the hurt
Taking the swallow, taking the drowning tank, taking the monster swell

Until the onslaught ebbs away, and the laughter of children
Ready to play again, sounds the all clear...

CROUTONS IN MY BELLAROM

You never stop worrying about the kids, young or old
They're your morning coffee and profiterole
They'll clean out your fridge and your bank accounts
Hung over, head down in a Weetabix bowl

Our girl was born on the first day of the IRA Ceasefire
So she's called Julia *Hope* to commemorate
The Shawshank Redemption also debuted Sept 1994
Another miracle release & inspirational date

So twenty-eight years later, I'm battling with croutons
Products of one *Bellarom Latte Blend* sachet
She left them behind along with so many other things
When she went back to the big choke today

Life's lumpy when you've the responsibility of children
Restraint, interventions; how to comprehend
You're on your knees for no-fees, Catholic education
Thereafter hope health and happiness blend

Our JuJu is living in Walthamstow with her new beau
Daniel and his cool family, Lindsay and Jude
We're looking forward to discussing strategy with LJ
How to handle our devilish handsome brood

When the kids fly the coup, you're left weirdly bereft
A limbless flibbertigibbet blathering on Skype
So we comfort ourselves with photos of Bella couple
And look forward to *lumps* of a different type...

For our Daughter JULIA HOPE

WAVING OFF THE LAST BUN SPECIAL

The 8ᵗʰ of May, 2020 is this coming Friday, 75ᵗʰ Anniversary of VE Day
The Allied Victory over Nazi Germany, ending England's World War II

Farewell to life in Holborn Underground Station and the Bun Specials
Supply Trains carrying 5,000 tons of food from six depots every day
Over 170,000 shelterers sleeping with their children and loved ones
On stilled wooden escalator steps and makeshift rail-track bunk-beds
Huddled in blankets on platforms where the stale air blew, secretly...

Bunker safe from the Blitz Monster on the Streets of London up above
The Luftwaffe battering the Capitol, faceless doodlebugs cutting out
And come the morning after, homes in flames, bodies in rubble-ruins
Back to work on the first tube rumble at six - keep calm and carry on...

Mrs. Mary Ramsey of Betterton St. Convent Garden serves her final
Cup of tea from a watering can, waitressing a last twopenny meal
Or a cup of hot cocoa with sausage rolls and freshly made sticky buns
Everyone banding together during the onslaught and national crisis
As aunts midwifed babies, while some old-uns never reopened eyes

And here we are 75-five years later in a lock-down of a different sort
Another heartless monster raging at us, but this time, in lung droplets
Inside ill-prepared care homes and full hospitals with tubes ventilators
Coronavirus Covid-19, disease-scything the defenceless and vulnerable

Quarantine has felt like the end of the world, and of our own making
And yet at other times, it's been a chance to regroup and prioritise life
Will we maybe miss the camaraderie and looking out for each other?
Will we clap hands on porches for frontline staff and NHS heroes again?

75-years ago in the May sunshine with their kit no longer dirtied by war
British Troops formation marched into the liberated city of Copenhagen
Forward smiling as they held heads high for the fallen who couldn't
Cheered on by a 1945 populace trembling with freedom and gratitude

And back home, Impatient for the end and a day to proper celebrate
"When Will The Victory Bells Ring Out?" screamed the paper headlines
As they do now, longing for social-distancing and uncertainty to end...

But will we learn from our mistakes, death-statistic history repeat itself as
Another monocled, test-tube marauder lays waste to all that is good...

Will we once again wave off a last bun special leaving a train depot?
Bound for the weary masses, hope and sustenance for sheltering folk

Looking to the powers that be for leadership in a crass rudderless boat
A disease-proof safe haven for those stranded out there in the kill zone

Who never want to hear that shrill, siren warning go off, ever again...

RED SQUIRRELS

Bursting into firehose-life from a crafty well-camouflaged stillness
It's been 38-years since I've seen your pointed impish puss
Scurry and skit across slippery moss and twigs and silver torso pines
Back when I was a lone Irish youth-hosteller nudging twenty-two...

Yank-introduced Grey Squirrels hunted down too-nice hoards of Reds
Across neat garden trestles, secure riverbanks and countryside England
Where only the canniest fighters survived the shapeless manmade cull

But not apparently in The Kilmacurragh Botanical Gardens in Wicklow
On a glorious September 2018 Irish day where an impossibly cute furball
Goads our holidaying shuffles with red-glimpses from only yards away...

A cairn of stones marks the new resting place of seventh-century monks
Their graves uprooted by crass estate owners in the 50ts for a tennis court
Even now the head-gardener will not wander
In that part of the woods at night (or any night)
Where aching spirits haunt gnarly-roots and rope-twisted trunks
Angry soil still churning deep below the so-dignified acceptance...

Our family pounded with heart disease and cancers these last few years
My younger sister Cathy answered her front door in Dublin yesterday
Her tearful post-chemo body bruised and battered and tissue-gowned
Me standing there flummoxed, wishing I'd amounted to more financially
So I could at least ward off the creepy shadow of serious ill health...

But I'm standing amidst giant redwoods, thick yews and hydrangea trees
With our impossibly upbeat tour-guide Angela enthusiastically explaining
About life and death and nature's countless re-flowerings and re-births...

When I see Mr. Red's irrepressible fidget-face reappear up to our left
Survival coursing through his genetically hot-wired limbs and adapted skin
Marking a dart for it while the coast is clear and the new day sun blinds...

Racing onwards and upwards
Skimming over long needles and jagged bark
Up onto another second-chance branch
Atop a centuries-old sycamore tree
Where the bastard shadow cannot reach...

For my Sister CATHY in Dublin

BADGE OF DISHONOUR
(Licking The Abyss)

Complicity and appeasement no longer hugs the shadows
Like the good old days of shush and do-not-engage
Instead they peacock allegiances; my badge of dishonour
Mussolini head-nod the filmed arrogance & fay rage

We've just witnessed a British Prime Minister outed by media
Trivial technicalities exploited, hysterical morality bull
Now Boris Johnson is standing outside No.10 Downing Street
Clutching a resignation speech, explain away a cull

But the Pro Europeans have hammered away at CakeGate
While a retaliatory BeerGate sickened the populace
Both childish leaders as buffoonish as their bloviate promises
To bring England back to glory, post pandemic muss

Boris did himself no favours by giving the non-stories oxygen
Apologizing, when he should have crushed these lies
Lead and don't talk about leading, build and be rebuilding
Instead of chasing the tail of this diversionary disguise

For someone who promised a better Britain and real growth
He ended up defending a concerted campaign ruse
Delivered the promised Brexit, survived Covid and had a kid
Only to throw away his premiership, an avoidable lose

But the worst part has to be the against-our-decision deriders
Looking out for their career as the ship licks the abyss
And now we're left with inflation, fuel hikes and a broken NHS
Cakes and beers and elected officials taking the piss

In 2022, we face a future riven with environmental destruction
We have maybe 25 to 30 years to finally take control
But all we get are self-interest lobbies and hurt conglomerates
Spinning truth, fucking us over, future in a septic hole...

SQUEEZING OUT SPARKS
WITH GRAHAM PARKER IN STOCKHOLM

I'll never forget when Rolf Borg (yes that surname) assured me
The train into *Stockholm* would arrive at precisely 10:23
He'd holidayed in Dublin and met his bride (my friend) Angela
But he also knew that Irish transport was cack (tee hee)

So I stood on the *Järfälla* platform and sure as God made poo
In rolls the stock, doors open, punters exit; new ones in
So we're heading into Sweden's capitol city on 7 August 1979
I even see half of Abba in a Volvo, fat chauffeur's grin

Slowing for the next stop, he points to a broken platform clock
And smiles; will be fixed this afternoon when we return
And as sure as Satan made the flimsy roof to contain the khazi
Later it functioned correctly, harmonious hours to burn

Even back then, Swedes paid a boatload more personal taxes
A Socialist Government repaying with logjams cleared
But I found it all clinical and detached and just so fucking cold
I longed for my Dublin where actual efficiency is weird

I was lucky to angle a ticket for Graham Parker and The Rumour
Stood there as his band debuted *Squeezing Out Sparks*
Thinking about the carved communal Chess Sets left out at night
They'd be petrol-doused in Dublin; toast in public parks

Over the decades I've recounted their staggering social services
How everything utilized their natural resources of wood
But I still can't decide if visitor-shoes-off for someone else's home
Is bollox or behavioural pointers that could do us good

So I think about all those gorgeous Master Race Swedish Blondes
Looking like Anni-Frid and Agnetha in Mamma Mia prime
And wonder why Irish Angela left Dirty Dublin for Spick Stockholm
When she could have had my ragged shamrock sublime...

For ANGELA and ROLF BORG and THE CHILDREN OF THE REVOLUTION

BENCHING BARRY WHITE
(Langers and Mash)

It's 1974 and *Be Thankful For What You Got* by William DeVaughn
Is played by the lurve-DJ - craftily slowing down the mood
You've summoned up Herculean courage, asked cutie to dance
Pulled her close, but *Langer Alert,* up pops something rude

Painfully aware of your involuntary macho libido in a public place
You panic as she chuckles, registering your motivated poke
The Saints of International Piety are demanding jail without parole
For your lack of propriety over that infernally excitable yoke

You hazard a kiss and find that's its bliss and suddenly you're hard
Where once in swimming pools, Percy was cruelly berated
Now the mere sight of a smock, Levi bum or lamb's wool tank top
And your once sedate Johnson, is most acutely stimulated

Soon you're all *Langers & Mash*, jumping up and down in car seats
Fumbling with bra-straps in a fleapit matinee showing Jaws
You've a stain on your corduroy that isn't a Cadbury's Fry's Crème
Where your faucet was encouraged to obey nature's laws

Several fathers have formed vigilante groups and flown out to Sicily
Where they were eagerly taught tooth and nail extractions
Next time you go near *their blemishless*, it won't be a horse's head
But something south of *your* border, ceasing all transactions

Flicking a wah-wah guitar, digging the scene with a gangster lean
Here comes another sister with her bellbottoms on just right
But who's that behind her with an axe and fourteen industrial pliers
Maybe I'll turn off the turntable - and *Bench My Barry White...*

NO PAROLE FROM THE INFINITE SCROLL

Aza Raskin is the tech-inventor of the never-ending *Infinite Scroll*
That *Facebook*, *Twitter* and *TikTok* unashamedly employs
The Razzer has apologized for wasting just over 200,000 lifetimes
Flicking up and down screens on hand-held mobile toys

Social Media and The Internet now dominate all communication
And it's impossible for most of us to cold turkey this tease
We've ending up posting shit-tons of naff snaps and declarations
Trying to illicit validation-honey from a nest of loony bees

Our need to be seen as authentic has turned us all into peddlers
Working the emotional testimonials and fictitious display
We're competing in a popularity contest rigged by algorhythms
That somehow knows what our brains want others to say

But for all its detractors and Digital Big Brother watching-warnings
The Net has also rejoined us with many forgotten friends
Connections and affirmations make us all feel a little less isolated
Positive footage is healing and laughter pays dividends

So I'm cool with a scroll down old Memory Lane (and Penny too)
As I trawl the megahertz looking for the newest online hit
And should I stumble on a former lover from bachelor bedsit days
We'll laugh about Catholic guilt and turning the other tit

So take me as you find me, my worldwide web of rational minds
Keep your panties from tangles and knickers out of knots
I'm off to post a video of my magnificent contributions to poetry
Before we're all uploaded by megalomaniacal A.I. bots...

EMILY BLUNT'S BATH WATER
(Embracing Allure)

I've been reading Clive James and his books of poetry
Chomping down on the raconteur every night
His fabulous wit and honesty seep through the crafted
Especially towards the end, CJ facing the light

Like all men of a certain age, Clive adored hot ladies
And name-dropped a famous beauty or three
Catherine Zeta-Jones, Angelina Jolie and Kate Mara
Sexed up actioners, misters slavering helplessly

Clive writes about them with wonder and boyish grin
But detractors would be quick to call him goat
The joyless media bigs up such guttersnipe responses
Failing to see what made gals so float his boat

The worship of Goddesses is hardly a shocking reveal
They've been casting their spell since the start
But I suspect it was the gumption and go-getter burn
That really moved our Clive, admiration impart

For me it's always been Emily Blunt, an English actress
The Ems'ser is gorgeous and can do no wrong
I'd literally drink her bath water and declare it Merlot
An aromatic bouquet of life-replenishing pong

Emily has a husband now and two beautiful children
Irritant details I choose to conveniently ignore
And like Clive James I will watch the talented A-lister
Continue to flourish on brave decisions galore

Are we drawn to the unattainable like flaying moths?
Seeking out the heat we know we cannot get?
Or is it that theirs is a path, we could have sought out
Had we found the courage, jettisoned the net?

I read in his final verses, a man still giddily enamoured
Their life force and beauty and talent; it thrilled
Not just the sculpted physicality Gods had gifted, but
They *embraced their allure*; then a future willed...

HIP BONES CONNECTED TO THE THIGH BONES
(*The Prisoner* Finale)

There were few TV programmes hammered like *The Prisoner*
It blew my newly impressionable Irish teenage mind
It was weird, mad, sexpot brilliant and had striped umbrellas
And a wobbly balloon that suffocated from behind

Mod types drove round *The Village* in Mini Moke open-tops
A Village Map pointed you to your housing location
But the place is full of mindless and indoctrinated automats
Names replaced by a low numerical denomination

Actor Patrick McGoohan plays an English Agent who retires
Raging at his London handler, a kit car speeds away
But he's soon gassed at home by a midget butler, wakes up
Incarcerated in a dominion where none can disobey

Each episode was a game of subterfuge and mind fuckery
The script exploring compliance, culling of human will
And every week No. 6 would greet the latest No. 2 nemesis
Orwellian efforts to break 'Six' with pal trickster overkill

As the series went on, McGoohan flexed wild artistic license
Making the sweep of The Prisoner's journey mentalistic
But when its Finale had a loony jury singing about Hip Bones
He fled the country when incensed fans went ballistic

Decades of speculation have followed since its 67/68 airing
And McGoohan desisted in any proper explanation
I think as he finally uncovered the mask to No. 1 (it's himself)
He meant that part of you that bows to capitulation

This provoking Cult TV Show now enjoys worldwide adoration
Even had a remake that didn't quite hit dizzy heights
But I think it's about our individuality being sneakily corroded
That spooked Pat into *protecting such precious rights...*

For PATRICK McGOOHAN and his Numbered Crew
And all groundbreaking TV Shows ever since

REPLACING LONGING UNSAID
(Our Joyful Gaggle of Shouters)

Back in the 90s day, I was lost to the world when we became friends
Pure solid gone if you thought my latest bad joke remotely funny
I'd watch in awe as you arranged wild flowers in cool ceramic vases
Bought at local E17 market stalls with subsistence day-job money

We'd peruse teeshirt rails and hand-carved wooden-spatula utensils
Knick-knack imbibing your flat with homely Feng Shui installations
Trying not to look like Mr. Blobby loons with string tufts of Candy Floss
As we juggled with other people's glorious homemade creations

There was a Kindergarten Pre-School on Fleeming only a few doors up
And in the morning you could hear the wall of kiddy play and joy
Screaming their pink lungs out with the abandon of prisoners let loose
Life coursing through every vivacious tomboy girl and giddy boy

Sat in the garden sunshine on a blanket with bottles of cheap bubbly
Two pals are hoot calling on myriad previous relationship mistakes
Then your tie-dye outfit hit the bedroom floor that instinctual evening
And bubbling-under tremors erupted into possibility's earthquakes

Health issues may have taken the 32-year dairy off of our present days
And the inevitable old-age scrap for survival sniggers on up ahead
But I thank the great hospital slap of life for ushering in new beginnings
When *our joyful gaggle of shouters* replaced all that longing unsaid...

For our three Children – DEAN, JULIA HOPE and SEAN FRANCIS

AND AS MUCH HEART

Mary Ann is crying uncontrollably at the wheel of our stationary car
Purging pain that's been building up inside her mother's soul for years

We've just left the Westgate *Carlton Cinema* on a sodden Monday
Matinee packed for *The Guernsey Literary & Potato Peel Pie Society*
A beautiful film about book clubs, World War II and the power of love
Actress Lily James and Dutchman Michael Huisman gold as the leads

But my wife of sixty isn't thinking about the island's Hovis Advert scenery
The bravery of those under occupation vs. the capitulation of snakes
The rapidly evacuated children shuffling confusedly onto ships in 1940
Shoreside parents gritting their teeth, projecting *it'll be all right* faces
My pal is thinking about our boy as he sat with us in Screen 3's front row
Making inappropriate noises throughout the challenging screening
Unable to control his Autism as he giggled and blurted and twitched...

Will our vulnerable five-foot eight 26-year old ever have another's *love*?
Be loved back - have children of his own - know the beautiful legacy
Of union, extending out tall and brave, into their own limitless future
And yet on a day when the house renovations have sprung two leaks
Rainwater pouring down through years of roofing Bodge-it-and-go...
Buckets catching the deluge while the boys brave the winds and rain
I don't feel panicked or depressed or sullen like the bitch that snapped
At Dean for pushing open an electric door in the Special Needs Pool
I look at our boy with pride as his huge smile registers *I got through it*

Maybe he doesn't understand the Nazis and their extermination cruelty
The tiny pitch battles that punctuate decisions to break free of chains
Slithering insufferable jackboot monsters sneering at the body different
Whose slime-intolerance tried to history-shadow what they saw as lesser

But I think of Lily James running towards Michael Huisman on the docks
No matter what the odds, no matter what the obstacles thrown down
Determined to grab life, the love in her heart making it hard to breath
Lucky souls who've found each other, writ large on their lit-up faces
And that Jane Eyre quote still magical after all these centuries
So Inspired, and relevant, still illuminating...

"...Do you think because I'm poor, obscure, plain, and little
I am soulless and heartless? You are wrong!
I have as much soul as you! And full as much heart!"

I LOVE TRACEY EMIN AND TRACEY EMIN LOVES ME

Does it take a trip to the edge of physical and terminal destruction
For us to finally see the preciousness of our only life
And how cavalierly we squandered the starting blocks afforded us
Because health and responsibility equated to strife

Neither money nor fame gives you back what you almost forfeited
Sap moves you knew were fool, but paid no heed
It's been nearly tens years and I'm still haunted by slender escape
Came far to close to leaving loved ones to bleed

There's a graffiti on the Margate cliff walls scribbled in white chalk
Declaring for our local hero of seaside regeneration
I Love Tracey Emin And Tracey Emin Loves Me it wittily broadcasts
The local artist that became a world-class sensation

But by way of making her ordeal contribute to our understanding
She has explained why appreciating life so matters
We take for granted minor physical abilities and mental cognition
Until the hammer of cancer cudgels all into tatters

So here's to the fighters and their unmade beds and tortured work
Here's to the ones who splash their passion on walls
Because I want to be in their numbers, hold a keyboard up proud
When scythe actually is making his judgement calls...

For TRACEY EMIN
And all the artists who survived Pandemic in the city
Then flocked to the coast

TWO WEEKS AWAY

Fighting for supremacy in my elephantine intellect
An army of prepositions and antonyms wrestle
I generously let them use my name as a reference
As they seek out a grammatical artistic vessel

With statuesque verbiage and fantastical pronouns
I will drive quockerwodger disbelievers away
The only formality holding up my global domination
Is working out what it is, I actually plan to say

I'm always two weeks away from finishing the book
That will reveal my genius to the piddly masses
They'll swoon at my prodigious cranial delectations
If M.B. Yeats could only find his reading glasses

Nor shall I engage in glib disingenuous empiricisms
For the sake of rolling out gorgonized phrases
No manure on the roses of my learned cogitations
Sprouting prestigious in glittering poetic vases

I sooth myself knowing that my callipygian genius
Is now as sought after as a CD by Kula Shaker
While I'm at home doing a sluberdegullious syntax
Up the back passage of its meritorious maker...

For WRITERS, ARTISTS, EGOTISTS and LEFTFIELD SOULS everywhere

DESK CLERK DRESSED IN BLACK

"Hail! Hail! Rock and Roll! Deliver me from the days of old!"
Chuck Berry sang on Chess Records, all was saved
But it was the King who rescued us from decorous dances
His "Heartbreak Hotel", all gyrating and depraved

I framed the 78" for HMV POP 182 in its gorgeous label bag
Protecting the British ten-inch shellac disc, so brittle
My "All Shook Up", "Hound Dog" and "Blue Suede Shoes"
Have pride of place on my wall too, lick and spittle

Keith Mowser was a customer of mine at Reckless Records
Remembered hearing Elvis Presley conquer his street
A pal of his had the record and was blasting its dark magic
Out through the window directly to his post-war feet

Keith's face always filled up with joyousness at the thought
Of that stunning sound; been solid gone ever since
Suddenly everything seemed possible in his drainpipe work
A Rock 'n' Roll record made every pauper a Prince

In 1956 we were all from a musical town called Squaresville
It was a sharp right turn, heading south of Hick City
Where freckles, Lawrence Welk Waltzes and flat Crew Cuts
Were deemed to be wholesome, polite and pretty

Protect us Lord from Great Balls of Fire and A-Wop Bopping
And Three Steps To Heaven charting their mortal sin
Establishment blew a gasket when Rock & Roll bust through
And suddenly it was us and not them that could win

So here's to the King of Rock & Roll who saved the teenager
From the tyranny of narrow-minded musical cack
Because every time I eye those framed HMV 78's on my wall
I ache with pride at our desk clerk dressed in black...

For ELVIS PRESLEY who saved us all (and fan KEITH MOWSER)

IDEA PANACEA (Higher Ground)

When Extra Terrestrial Intelligence finally reveals itself
Their elliptical sphere on the Whitehouse Lawn
Explaining how they seeded Humanity with gene ick
Spliced into the pool at our evolutionary dawn

As they disembark in blobules, will they be impressed
Or thumb-downs what millennia has produced
Explaining to all how loser-cancerous Homo Sapiens
Reverts to primordial soup, terminally reduced

Sorry you were preoccupied with accumulating dross
And to the irrevocable collapse of life so blind
Shake a can of spray paint, and splatter alien graffiti
"Goodbye Cruel World and Moronic Mankind!"

We are teetering on the brink of physical annihilation
Fussing over actors with a junkie need for fame
We need to find a cure-all for our children's children
Who need answers, not an allocation of blame

We've all seen the global bush fires and glide icecaps
As the news reports yet more soil-erosion abuse
But what scares the living shit out of me is our duplicity
Another politician with his oily plausible excuse

We pin our hopes on a Klaatu-type Universal Remedy
Cleverly fix the environmental apocalypse anon
Maybe a genius like Elon Musk invents *Idea Panacea*
That staves off the lead-up to our Earth's oblivion

We must develop and implement renewable energy
Into a teensy device costing less than a dime
But if our generation has access to stellar information
Why are we so complacent with so little time?

It's a beautiful thought that solutions will simply come
From masters keeping a celestial watchful eye
But I fear it'll be that other bulbous Acid Head hissing
As we scrabble for lost higher ground, and die...

THE BURDEN of GREATNESS
(Oscar in the Afterlife)

There's an Irish postcard dedicated to Oscar Wilde
Showing his photo and his tenure on Earth
Between 1854 and 1900, he dazzled all academia
With plays and quotes of legendary worth

From *"I have nothing to declare except my genius"*
"I can resist everything except temptation"
On to *"Be yourself, everyone else is already taken"*
Each was erudite, refined, a sassy creation

But his sexual peccadilloes scandalized old society
And on a liable case, paid a terrible price
The burden of greatness came down on him hard
For acting on his famously self-wise advice

Now a celebrated wit beloved across generations
The gutter man who looked up at the stars
Us still taking from the importance of being earnest
As we lose worlds of prejudicial prison bars

He said some cause happiness *wherever* they go
Whenever they go applied to the ugly rest
So I see our Oscar walking afterlife with a partner
Exuding talent, in his puffed out hero chest...

For our friends TED ROGERS and JARRED HENDERSON
For OSCAR WILDE and all the Oscars

A SENSE of SPITFIRES

Mary Ann and I are sitting on a lovingly kept remembrance bench
In the truly gorgeous coastal town of St. Margaret's at Cliffe in Kent
Lolling in a specially carved out grass verge with breathtaking views
Scoffing down homemade tuna sandwiches with a chunky cup of Tea

On a sunny October day, it overlooks the now settled English Channel
France's coastline clearly visible in the miniscule twelve-mile distance
People Ferries and Cargo Tubs trundling into Dover Harbour on the right

You can feel the peace and tranquillity, the calm heart of the place
The white cliffs below the near horizon and nature buzzing all around
Wild lavender on the roadside with hidden crickets in the hedgerows
And even in momentary silences - a sense of Spitfires...

Mary Ann gets silly and does a Victory Roll down the grass incline
An elderly couple in sensible shoes and beany hats chuckle nearby
So terribly British and utterly soppy after all these decades together

We decide on a walk up to the anchors of the Dover Patrol Memorial
Fading letters on a pointed monolith celebrating bravery and sacrifice
Money types own palatial sea-view homes on an idyllic Granville Road
With names like "Moonraker", "Skyfall", "Hope Point" and "The Haven"

A carved grass footpath amidst ploughed fields and swooping starlings
Lead to shaved-patch benches, the plunging cliff edge only feet away
Two pint-sized ponies, three wild horses and a lone ram share the gorse
While a bulbous black dung beetle shuffles across freshly laid poo-pats
An ancient strength pushing that vulnerable outer shell on and on...

You feel how little divided democracy from tyranny in those dark days
How those white sheers must have looked to the returning pilot lad
Guiding his symmetrical machine onto the grass of a pock-marked field
As the even younger crew run forward to greet him...

Cranky hospital nurses told us to snap out of our mooch and whine
To sit up and smell the roses, take in the sun and nature and fresh air
Both of us survivors of serious illness yards away from another precipice
Ghosts of the past guiding, perched on the shoulder, ear whispering...

And as a light breeze caresses our faces - I think that life is like a War
There's a time to good-fight and battle - a time to dig in and defend
Then there's a time to play and get jiggy and be proper rambunctious
A time to roll down hilly grass like you used to when you were a kid...

So both aged 60 and still relatively intact
We look up into the clear blue skies
Humbled, grateful, appreciative...

Savouring the tingle of freedom and survival
Filled with thanks and hope
And a sense of Spitfires...

JESUS IN THE SPAGHETTI

Jesus is in the Spaghetti Hoops with long hair and Turin face
And was recently seen in a Pizza, Pineapple & Ham
It wasn't Pol Pot, Stalin, Hitler, Caesar Augustus or Hannibal
Or even Russian-originated thought-control E-spam

It really is Christ in marmalade rinds on your buttered toast
The Saviour's image was on top of a curry sauce too
Or maybe it was people's overworked media imagination
Because no one knows what he looked like, no clue

The spiritually enlightened and their authoritarian disciples
Want us to worship at their altar, bow down to God
And if you don't concede to their hysterical indoctrination
May have to boot camp you, cleanse *your* evil bod

Why are we so easily conned into believing obvious dross
Like the ludicrous Scientologists, L. Ron Hubbard bull
A Science Fiction writer invents his money-spinning clique
And no one calls time on gullibility cups, running full

Jesus is not in caramelized sugar or aromatic Basmati rice
He's not staring up at us from Peruvian coffee beans
And when he walks into the Whitehouse, then Downing St.
He won't be grading portraits by resemblance means

He'll reiterate the simple truth, giving is a learned response
As every awkward love poem and song tries to tell
Stop looking for images of me in foodstuff/muslin scorches
And lose those dictatorial Ayrian broadcasts as well

Jesus is in the face of the woman building an orphanage
In the hands of a comforter amidst battered wives
Jesus is not in the cudgel or battering ram or suicide vest
Hidden beneath the true believers bloodshot eyes

Jesus is in the flesh of a newborn, the medals of veterans
Not walking on water, when there's soup to make
And if he's talking through groceries, here's his message
To love or not love is *your decision,* not *my mistake...*

GADFLIES RECANT

We came down to Margate to take a break in the play
Dump a piss-poor first-half for a better second act
And every day in the last five years is a feelings toss-up
Between what we've gained minus residue intact

You have to be thankful for any re-opened door to life
Find some form of sanctum; let old gadflies recant
It's just that as you walk by more gull-ripped offal bags
It's hard to stifle another slob-miscreants inner rant

Yet in the old town are youngsters dressed to the nines
Laughing and enjoying the seaside sun with chums
We sip overpriced lagers and ruminate on architecture
Enjoying the energy, not missing mortgaged drums

It's a strange transition between its former depravation
To renewal and gentrification everywhere you look
Sometimes we feel like observers; over-shoulder-readers
Looking into someone else's fantastical new book

You get so angry at your former-selves for chances lost
The spunk/cahonies needed for hard-battles won
But tonight, we sit listening to Ska Music outside Olby's
Laughing with skinheads & mods, tuned-in as one...

HORROR DEFLECTED

I've a vivid memory of not being allowed to go to a party
A ten-year olds birthday bash in our tiny cul-de-sac
Singled out by the backstabbers for some spurious reason
I bawled my kiddy eyes out, my first rejection attack

I remember an older guy, bit of a sadistic mouth almighty
Picked up a cat in an empty schoolyard by its tail
And in front of me, he pretended to sling it over the brick
But it smashed into the concrete, died after a frail

Alan was a friend who'd been sunbathing on the Bull Wall
Woke up and without checking, dived in head first
I watched in horror like everyone else as the stretchers left
Broke his neck, wheelchair bound, agile to nursed

When my Mum lost John Wolfe at only 58, I was under ten
I'd never seen such pain as she wept for her Dad
I felt so helpless, as nothing I said or did, eased her misery
Her parental safety net gone, a child alone, sad

Someone she'd looked up to had been casually stricken
Random inane decisions with huge consequences
All through life, it's been a lottery, get lucky or get tanked
Never knowing which one will start in on the senses

'There but for the grace of God go I...' commonly recited
A catchall out-clause for all that horror deflected
I just hope that our children get better life mentors than us
A future where vulnerables are cruelty-protected

Looking over our little world in the vastness of open space
Who pulls the lever on our cosmic-puppet machine?
Which person gets to live a full life, walk tall, build legacy?
While the unluckiest pull casualties of the obscene?

When I sleep, sometimes I dream of people from the past
And wonder why some got the breaks, others not?
But I've also learned to wake up early, and dress the part
And be damn respectful for *what I've actually got...*

LEE 4 DONNA vs. BILLY NO MATES
(Chalk Hearts)

*"Fuck The Tories! Welcome To The Shitish Isles!
We All Live In A Simulation and I'm Gonna Download Your House!"*

Now that it's sunny and the sea-wind-howl
Isn't biting off your knob and shrivel sack
The Da Vinci Code Graffiti Kids of Margate have been letting it rip

They zap surfaces with the clumps of white chalk
Crumbled indecorously downwards off the cliff walls
Where world-class sonic erosion has worn away centuries
Of people carvings and homing nests...

I remember being that intense once
When we were young and hot to snot
Swearing blind to causes, down on your beliefs
Buoyed with a burning righteousness
Gouging out our rad ideas and genuinely heartfelt allegiances
Into suburban facia...

LEE 4 DONNA
Is painted on a back-garden wall in Gordon Road
But will he love his Donatella tomorrow, be there for the Donster
When her Shirelles moment comes roaring in?

On the same gentrified suburban backwater
There's a preppy DFL-type in her late-twenties
Full-term *Down From London* pregnant, petting her huge tummy
Standing with her uncomfortably redundant partner
Outside a converted townhouse door
Yacking with a friend over by the wall and entrance gate
Discreet social distancing, unspoken

Preggers looks eager to drop (and I mean eager)
But is also worried about this Nationally notorious *Covid-19 Hot Spot*
Thanet Hospitals consistently being overrun and unable to cope

Will there even be a safe bed - a burly earth-mama midwife
That's actually able to do her crucial job
Cumbersome PPE encroaching her jellied-eel gloves
And will her bewildered-looking beau properly man-up come the gore
As even the halos of saints is tested by the bip-crazed monitors

She protectively up-pulls on her bump
Up-pull, up-pull, over and over...

When I had a Dublin 21ˢᵗ Birthday party in 1979
Back in the sea-view hills of a Howth Head amenable Hotel
There were hundreds of friends there and even more stragglers
School-buddy Raymond 'Gally' Kelleher
Gave me a Brass Mead-Like Drinking Tankard
With an engraving *Congratulations from Ray & Lorraine*
It sits in my man-cave more than four decades old
Dusty and faded - Gally's in Australia now with someone else
Lorraine moved on too, and nowadays
Billy No Mates can count his friends on one hand and less...

An over-thinking conspiracy theorist
Has scrawled *Plandemic 2020-2021* on the footpath
(Underlining the pun on Pan)
Claiming we're half a cluster-fuck away
From a deliberately created man-made oblivion

So I smile at Lee and his undoubtedly cute-as-a-button Donsterina
And even though my once wild-moments may be mere memory now
And the tide of time remains ravage-relentless

I like the idea that I still want to reach for the quills of expression
My declarations of hope and love
Two-fingering the coming shit-storm

Still dodging that horrible shrieking gull of fate
That excrement-Stuka circling up above

Waiting for just the right moment to swoop down
On the dreams of chalk hearts...

CENTRE STAGE

Is it a form of unpalatable arrogance to take Centre Stage
Get up there and broadcast yourself to the masses
Or is it simply easier to sit paralyzed, back of the auditorium
Poo-pooing away such hubris, all gator and gasses

We fear looking foolish and ridicule those who take chances
Cannot be seen as an exhibitionist, egos untoward
Yet we go to plays and shows and concerts, heart pumping
As other souls fall daily on art's cruel arbitrary sword

Our youngest is pursuing his dreams of songwriter and actor
Constantly damning the critic torpedoes homing in
But take it from your Pops who procrastinated ad nauseam
Radar out all the cautionary, only gutsy gets the win...

For SEAN FRANCIS

JUST LIKE ALL OF US
(Does David Cassidy Need Love?)

Thinking about 1971 to 1974, my two Sisters and our hair-raising clothes
Back when Donkey Jackets and Monkey Boots were called *clobber*
Frances and Cathy in embroidered cheesecloth smocks and Wrangler
Bellbottoms that vied for attention with my epic Levi's elephant flares...

Days when I sneaked their weekly teen mag *Jackie* for tokenism pics of
Genesis and Yes, Peter Gabriel and his rad semicircle Prog Rock haircut
Bowie's Aladdin Sane paint-face and Keith Emerson's keyboard banks
Ian Hunter's Mott The Hoople frizz-hair and dude trademark sunglasses

Back when yuck-faced legions of Pop's pretty boys like David Essex and
Donny Osmond and the cute ones in Arrow, Pilot, Mud and Dawn sang
And sussed *Jackie* knew us older brothers were scoping *Real Life Stories*
For a head's up on what really made incomprehensible cool-girl's tick...

But had no earthly defence against the ultimate fantasy/fanny inducer
The Partridge Family's *David Cassidy*, who sent every single hot female
In the known universe into G-spot frenzies we lads could only dream of
Knicker-wetting eblutions and vocal dexterity not heard since fab 1964

And no longer reading *Judy, Bunty for Girls* or *Mary, Mungo and Midge*
Agony Aunts Cathy and Claire answered the wet outpourings of hotties
Suddenly finding teacher John Alderton just *so attractive* in *Please Sir!*
And although not *Alias Smith & Jones* hot like Ben Murphy & Peter Duel
Even 11-year old Danny Bonaduce might get a look in for being near...

Dear Cathy and Claire...
Does David plan to visit Hull, Skegness or perhaps even The Wirral soon?
Could he write a personal message on my *Could It Be Forever* sleeve?
Does David get his sexy smile from Movie Dad Jack or TV Mum Shirley?
Does he really chase after rainbows for someone to call his very own?
Just like all of us...

And if he can come down to our tent on the verge by his London Hotel
We'll share our Three-In-One Vosene bottle after his long flight to the UK
And I'll wear my scoop-neck dress with patch pockets and I'll keep my
Complexion fresh with Pond's Moisturising Cream and Clearasil Lotion
And my best friend Jess has promised me her etched Cowboy Boots...

Tell David that Jess and I regularly use IMMAC like *Babs* in *Pan's People*
And that Slade and Sweet and T. Rex and The Rollers don't interest me
And that I'll love horses too as soon as I escape the city for the country
Where we're not surrounded by so many people, pushing and shoving

Does he need Scalextric tips or perhaps even a Raleigh Chopper part?
There's room now 'cause my nut brother's after a sexy foreign student
That I know David would never be interested in or ever visit her country

I can even give him my scrapbooks with pencil drawings and cut outs
Of *Cherish, Rock Me Baby, How Can I Be Sure?* And my die-cut copy of
Dreams Are Nuthin' More Than Wishes still has his child painting inside...

Does David like sunsets? Does David's beautiful long hair get split ends?
Does David smile down at fans, street serenading him outside the BBC?
Does he think about England at home on his Partridge Family Tour Bus?

Is David really looking for someone to marry, looking for a special girl?
Looking for someone to have and hold and protect and be protected
Open spaces where we can walk his gorgeous shaggy dog together?

Do you think David could settle here in the UK instead of California?
Does he think Stacy Dorning in Black Beauty is pretty (I look like her)?
Does David mean it when he sings those beautiful songs on telly?

Please tell me Cathy and Claire - please tell me...
Does David Cassidy need love?
Just like all of us...

In memory of DAVID CASSIDY, April 1950 to November 2017
And BERNADETTE WHELAN, a fan that died in a stage crush
At his 27 May 1974 Concert in London, aged 14
And for our MARY ANN who was a huge fan and was at the gig

OUR MOMENT

From Wickford in Essex, I'm on the slow train
Bound for Liverpool Street, heading towards you
Petite farmlands neck with thorn and bramble
The wild and the tamed blending into one

And I'm thinking about how everything in Nature
Is either connected or connecting
How the way of Nature can mirror people sometimes
Beautiful, when it all falls into place

I'm going over the magic parts of last night
When you looked so young at heart, so wired into life
As I sat on your tall kitchen stool like a besotted teen
Watching you arrange the flowers I'd brought in earlier
A mishmash of pink and purple Sweet Williams
Weeding out the suspect, keeping only the good
Wanting the combination to be just right

Songs get to me now too. They always have, but especially now.
And as the landscape passes by with light flitting on the reflective glass
I can see us both - a few days back - knees up on your cozy settee
Listening to *Shadow Hunter* - our new Davy Spillane CD on Tara

We'd seen him and his band live at The Irish Fleadh
In Finsbury Park only days earlier
His emotion-wrenching Uilleann Pipes wafting out
Across the open fields and the ecstatic crowd
Blowing everyone away with *The Host Of The Air*
A W.B. Yeats poem put to music, dreams of long dim hair, piping
A slow melody with the ache of ghosts and a hoped-for better future

And as the train pulls into Liverpool Street Station
I can hear still hear *The Host Of The Air* playing
And so clearly too, especially towards the end

As the Irish and English love song
Melts into the laughter of children...

For MARY ANN SIMMONS

BEING THERE

The bittersweet nature of parenthood is often slow revealing
The roller-coaster journey it took to get to this place
When we see off our daughter of 28 on the Kings Cross 17:48
A tear of gratitude trickles down her beautiful face

Tonight she'll be back in Walthamstow with her doting beau
Laughing with his parents about movies, footy results
We wave off at a station; they stand smiling at a porch door
Both sets of grown-ups, proud of their evolving adults

And I'm reminded of my own Mum and Dad at Dublin Airport
How suddenly touched I was at their implacable care
Julia texts her Mum, she shed a tear in her carriage, because
We *both* showed up, when only one needed be there...

For our kids – JULIA HOPE, SEAN FRANCIS and DEAN

LEFTFIELD SOULS

Betwixt your mild-mannered kooks and stark raving mad
Lies the inhospitable domain of the artistic loon
Exhibitionists and code-warriors for next generation tech
Geek anarchic visionaries howling at the moon

No amount of reasoning can dissuade the wordy variant
As they tap on cake-engrained computer keys
Documenting the Illuminati, Pop and erectile dysfunction
Overdrafts, ample bosoms and toasted cheese

Pondering the Universe and unavailable leggy secretaries
They memorialize hope and epic emotional fails
Invent dual cyclone hoovers and banana flux capacitors
In spatter-paint overalls, chewing inky fingernails

It's often said that both genius and art is on the spectrum
And only the nutjobs have such an obsessive bint
You have to be arrogant, delusional or chop off your ear
Fix your one-track-mind, whilst permanently skint

But I prefer to say our compulsive-expressive *leftfield souls*
Aren't erratic nor egghead nor even Dr. Strange
They're just a luckier launch of boundless-ideas-rocketship
Blessed with an infinite palette, vision and range

The ones who push us forward have always been weirdos
Got monkey on my back and mania in the brain
And it's us that are delusional who think society normalcy
Isn't the worst kind of lunacy and *properly insane...*

For (DJ) BARNABY, Dancer TED ROGERS
And GHOST PAPA Record Shop and Staff (Margate)

SHINING THROUGH

Every Friday is Face Time on the iPhone with our boy Dean
A one-on-one with his pals and housemates Stephen and Nathan
And their carers - Morelia, Rachel, Friedar, Sophie and Nico

I'm reminded of a Bruce Springsteen song I played to death in 1992
A year after Dean's birth and post his diagnosis of Autism
"Better Days"
The joyous opener to the album "Lucky Town"

I could feel it in my soul every time I indulged
The music – the lyrics
I knew the Boss had just become a Dad too
The awe-inspiring magic of it
Like me – he'd found his Living Proof...

After work I'd come home to Dean's difficult behaviour
My lovely lady's barely contained grief
The words neither of us could say
The hurt now given a bastard name

Yet in the job the next day
I'd play that song again
Needing the spirit lift
Mainlining my needle of Musical Hope
Our firstborn's beautiful face lingering in my mind
His unsullied soul – his naked vulnerability
And I'd stare ahead as I listened
Hiding the tears from my work pals in Reckless
Who by now knew *that look* and were kind enough not to say
"These are better days...better days come shining through..."

Mary Ann and I are nearly 60 now and 25 years down the line
Dean is resident in Nutley Hall in Uckfield in Sussex

Amidst giggles and excitement, the image shuffles into focus
And I think of summer and sunshine, I think of Spirits in living things
Butterfly Wings in Nutley Hall, filling the gardens
Flitting about the flowers, wind chimes tinkling in the trees...

We see our Dino beaming contentedly with his pals and carers
And a little bit of God's mercy, comes shining through...

THE WEIGHT OF THE WORLD

When I seized the day, an early morning complained
I hadn't made enough coffee to get past noon
Then a nearby Aberdeen Heifer became apoplectic
When its over-the-moon jump peaked too soon

Living my best life put the nose out of ten normal lives
And the stars I forgot to reach for, all felt ignored
When I asked the world the weight of its total tonnage
It looked violated, fatso mark on its dietary board

How many steps must I climb on a Stairway to Heaven?
Why is that major league fool suffering so gladly?
Can I believe anything out of the mouths of wild horses?
Or those three blind mice caning beats so badly

Is Lollipop a genuinely good name for any kind of ship?
And should I ask the tree where the apple fell
Will Thomas be absolutely upfront about his doubting?
Or the gold in the cave, make Aladdin unwell

Can I buy wattage to illuminate the moon's dark side?
A colour-coded source-map locating the Nile
Should I get thirteen desserts to follow The Last Supper?
Convince the Mona Lisa to finally crack a smile

If I hear another Dove Cry in Detroit, I'll puke for a week
Letting It Be only made Mother Mary feel crappy
And would Bo be so pervy as to peep in polite society?
And just what is making Larry so fucking happy?

Will Samson ever feel safe passing an Arabic Hair Salon?
Can an Eden whispering serpent ever be wise?
Is Lucifer ever going to make up with his God Almighty?
Could we program Estate Agents to not tell lies?

Life is complicated enough without me inverting clichés
So I asked Jesus one night; this is what he said
My advice is to walk alongside each other, not on water
And concentrate on raising flour, not the dead...

ANDY DUFRESNE and the FREEDOM RAIN

When I think of my younger sisters Catherine and Francis
We're always sat round the kitchen table, nattering
Our horrendous fashion picks, PI-charting old bedfellows
Followed now by health, too much body battering

Chewing the cud on slow sets, car seats and field snogs
And the albums we clung to like musical Eucharist
The illicit thrills post school lessons, clandestine hook-ups
French kissing, going further, our geek teenage list

We'd scream with laughter at olden car-crash choices
Hemlines, hair-dos and the endless fashion craves
Too many embarrassing nights pissed and on the razzle
Kebabs, chippies, sat in trendy nightclub enclaves

But no reminiscence was complete without fleapit tales
Hundreds of thrilling movies, imagination insane
Genuine Frontier Gibberish, Mel Brooks' *Blazing Saddles*
Or *A Bad Week To Quit Sniffing Glue* in *Airplane*

Scare-em-shitless *Shining*, *Alien* chest-busting acid gore
Right up to *Titanic*, *Gladiator* and *The Revenant*
Spectacle and heart always wins your undying affection
The gasp/roar of the audience, baddies recant

It's stayed with us all of our lives, a constant companion
Through the beautiful up of children, horrors too
Quoting phrases from classics & groundbreaking scenes
The stuff of life that film portrays; hopeful renew

We gravitate towards the light in life, same for the past
Reaching for that which touched a deeper part
We've always known they were more than just images
Of society outsiders trying to catch another start

I think of Andy Dufresne in *The Shawshank Redemption*
Escaped, his hands held up in the freedom rain
The release of a second chance, his journey reflected
And I'm glad to be with my sisters, glued again...

For my Sisters FRANCES and CATHERINE

STAY WITH US
(All The Way USA)

Media types love to give America and Americans a bad press
A nation of psychotic hillbillies flaunting bibles and guns
But I've never found them to be anything other than generous
Eager to show you they're not part of TV's clichéd ones

I was new into Aer Lingus Reservations, based at Dublin Airport
And I'd done my year, ready for cheap stand-by flights
For decades I dreamed of steaming subways in New York City
But I knew no one there, no bolthole after viewing sights

So imagine my astonishment at a return telex (remember those)
Forget rip-off central hotels! *Why don't you stay with us?*
Raun and Jerry Burnham had a dual apartment on West 16th St.
Walking distance to 5th, The Village, a Times Square bus

So I'd leave at noon on Thursday, a £10 return-ticket on a Jumbo
EI105 from Dublin via Shannon airport to New York's JFK
Watch movies and listen to cool playlists on cheap headphones
Took the Airport Express into Manhattan, wowser display

They were both singers and musicians, put out albums in '69/'70
And had a spare room full of recording equipment/bed
I got to stay with these fantastic sophisticates and two moggies
Went to dinner and gigs and bought records until I bled

American Express Travellers Checks and 3-buck exchange rates
Meant that everything was proper cheap, even after tax
I went to Madison Square Gardens; the 8th Ave garment district
Saw Chess' Bo Diddley in a bar, riff his red box shape axe

I had swordfish for the first time, went to Jersey looking for Bruce
Stood petrified in Liberty's head as the wind made it sway
Found a Sligo man on the view-floor of the Empire State Building
Who stamped your cent with a punch-hole for dollar pay

Queued up Saturday midnight with others by newsagents on 9th
See Sunday's *New York Times* supplements be assembled
Read this 13-bit beast over freshly squeezed Florida orange juice
A $2-breakfast with eggs over easy like a feast resembled

It's not all peaches and cream; murdering gunmen too often vent
And if you've no job or medical, life becomes really shitty
But Americans believe in the ethos of everyone having a chance
And that's always been a hope doctrine, tough but gritty

Because R&J knew writers and singers and off-Broadway risk takers
Our nights were filled with debate, politics; the latest craze
Soul, Funk, R&B, Rock, Punk and Alternative poured out of airwaves
Seemed like the future was limitless, colour replacing greys

But like all great countries, Americans are full of odd contradictions
The melting pot of the world is home to so many dictates
The pallor changes colour, codes and creeds on every hustle street
And you have to fight for your voice; silence the ingrates

We were sat in a half-empty haunt, when AIDS began dominating
Toilet-seat hysteria, hospital refusals, ads carved in stone
I vividly recall a Trans crying on the bottom step of a 4th Ave Brown
His face bloodied, worse than humiliated, he was alone

Remainder shops stayed open in Times Square almost to midnight
The street ladies, cart vendors and wild neon all casting
Washington Red Apples, Pineapple Pizza Slices and crusty bagels
The energy of it all is infectious, NYC minutes everlasting

But my fondest memories are the ones where we just shot the shit
Watching Crazy Eddie adverts, talking Ellis Island legacy
They were proud of their city's heritage of all-culture acceptance
Rooms full of literature, dinner guests accepting you/me

There's a deep-down-inside part of every European freedom kid
That knows America invites you onto the dancing floor
Instructed, opened; I knew I owed my US-buds more than thanks
As tears welled in grateful eyes, flying home on EI 104...

For RAUN AND JERRY BURNHAM and our times in New York

THREE-INCH RISING BUTTS

This is what it's like to be a parent...

Standing in the shadow-doorway of Scott's Junk Emporium in Margate
Waiting 45-minutes for staff to return from their old-school 1-pm lunch
To buy a matching pair of usable three-inch rising-butt door hinges
For the architrave recess of an old stripped-pine slab bought on spec...

It's a hot August 2021 summer day and the cool breeze of the sea
Takes the edge off the seagull garbage-strewn side-streets of CT9
The self-taught genius Lew from No. 3 next-door and clueless me
Have been going for hours now at the entrance-beast of Julia's room
A returning-daughter, who, like all her generation, can't afford rent

Cool Sean (our 2nd) and his new beau Nat, stayed two whole nights too
Self-obsessed, lost in their hand-held media – woke interrogation stares
To see if we old-farts display irksome unconscious-bias towards genders

Were we any different when we were 26 and 22 back in the misty day
Any less judgemental; ever gave a tiny grateful thought to *our parents*
Who spent every second of every day, working for us, planning ahead
Like we have for our three artisans - July 1991, Sept 1994 and Feb 1998...

So I'm rummaging through a huge and deep box of used door hinges
Knife; concealed; spring-loaded; ball-bearing barrels; pewter overlays
With £1 to £4 dirty white stickers labelled on every knackered-remnant
Looking for three-inch rising butts because 2 ½ inch ones are too small
Nothing but the best for our wandering sibs and their tomorrow-dreams
Of having a nice place to live, shared with someone you love...

So I dig deeper into the rust and detritus of the past
Driven to up-cycle this paint-gunged relic, to forge a better future
Match up the sanded wood, Baldwin hinge and porcelain doorknob
Into something both ancient and returned; made all shiny new again

Inlay another chapter of care and love and home improvements
Into life's constantly re-hung grooves...

For our daughter JULIA HOPE

AT THE RANDOM WHEEL
(Celebration Of Life)

There's a makeshift memorial by a landscape tree in Westgate-On-Sea
On the busy road into the tiny but beautifully kept Thanet seaside town
Photos of a dapper 14-year old lad whose light was taken far too soon
The heartfelt shrine still regularly tended by admirers some 4 years on

"Our Charlie..." hanging silver-worded pendants affectionately declare
Cool looking Charlie Richardson in his dark Tarantino-esque sunglasses
Who, on a Friday evening in November 2015, walking home with friends
Stepped out between 2 parked cars and a van at Beach Rd. Junction
Blameless driver with less than a second to react to a local blindspot

4th of June 2019 is two days away and the Sunday papers are filled with
75thAnniversary supplements of the 1945 D-Day Landings at Normandy
We're visiting the off-road 12th century town of St. Nicholas-At-Wade
On a gorgeous Sunday afternoon for their *Open Gardens* fundraiser

On a local park bench, we meet an unknown gent in his late eighties
Who without prompt begins regaling his first childhood memory of War
Mum and a feverish toddler, pram-parked at their Canterbury surgery
Then after hours of waiting, casually ordered to come back tomorrow
It'll be all right, next day will do - a slight delay won't harm him much...

Only hours later, Luftwaffe bombers flattened that street in Canterbury
And he stands there in front of us with the haunted look of a survivor
Wondering even now who was at the random wheel of those choices?
Was *He There But For The Grace of God* or cruel bureaucracy's fodder?

Sat amidst personal notes with rain-blurred ink under plastic protectors
A *Celebration of Life Ceremony* by classmates at King Ethelbert School
Nestles alongside things that mattered to a hip young 14-year old lad
His donated organs now giving some other teenager a chance at life

And I suspect you're smiling some place else, young Charlie Richardson
Watching over the hurt souls you left behind, energetic and free

And forgiving those at the random wheel
You're hugging the lives they turned to dust
Their loss washed away, surrounded now by light and love...

For CHARLEY RICHARDSON of WESTGATE and his Family

A CLEARANCE UP AHEAD

"...It's Stage 3 Breast Cancer..." - you said on the phone
Standing outside St. Barts Hospital in London rain

My jaw drops to the floor - dumbfounded – silenced
It feels like some badly played out home-cinematic moment
A marauder careering around the phone table in deafening 5.1
Assaulting all my senses with stupefying hurt...

Everything is statistics now; your markers are all numbers
It's *not* Stage 4, that's good you're told, four is lethal, you're told
Terminal in most cases - but your mind races to the inbetween
Stage 3 is *worse* than Stages 1 or 2 and it was initially only
A grizzled up inside-lump you found on your left breast one night
While watching a Syrian Mum trying to get into Britain
Cradling her sunken-eyed daughter

At least it can be treated when it was a death sentence years ago
There's an immediate scheduling of a mastectomy
Combined with DIEP reconstruction
Surgeons will cut out your stomach fat to refill the deflated breast
No stark flat space that way, no linear scar, no feminine nipple either
And the lymph nodes will have to come out too, infected...

You see, Cancer has no conscience, no feelings and no Godly mercy
Stage 4, won't be grinning at mountains of sideboard get-well cards
You'll be planning goodbyes, wills – using words like *legacy* and *passing*
Sobbing quietly at night on a ward full of hurt slashed women

And yet here you are post op - three sessions into the cudgel of Chemo
Hair all fallen out - bloated from the steroids that make you eat and eat
The 24-7 nausea making you wretch and vomit

Here you are, still standing, in your pyjama wrap
Picking at the mushroom omelette I made, in sickness and in health
No longer just overdone lines spoken at a ceremony for video proof

I look at you - weary – a slam-walled torso that's up against it
But then I'm breathless with love as you brave a smile and mention
That the rain is forecast to stop soon - will be a clearing up ahead...

For MARY ANN

THE OCEAN

It's all in the kiss, they say

Your first kiss was slightly awkward
In that crowded Soho bar
Jabbing to the Trevor Horn precision of *Owner Of A Lonely Heart*

Then days later
Eyeing grown-over initials on tree trunks in our local park
You took me again
And suddenly your kiss was like the warmth of the sun

I was scared too, wasn't I, as I always am
Should I go deeper into this bear-pit of open, this huge vulnerable
Find structure, solace, something to hold on to
When love offers no peace, no safety net, not really

And even now, even here in your arms at our friend's party
Where everyone knows us
I'm like some boat bobbing up and down on the vastness of the Sea
Water lapping at the perfectly polished veneer beneath
Soothing all on-board above

A sway that scares me witless
I'll sink, I'll sink, I swear I will, and I'll drown
And I never want to be out there again, drowning, sinking...

So I lean over, licks my lips in invite, and dive in regardless
And our two mouths collide into a sort of familiar storm
Into this crazy foolish falling and the soft cherish
And the lovely calm afterwards

I knew it the first time our lips met
In was in your face and mine
As we pulled back and sipped on our drinks casually
Acting as if nothing much had just happened

It's all in the kiss, they say
And yours is the Ocean...

A LONG WAY FROM KANSAS

It's a windy, but gloriously sunny Saturday afternoon in Margate Town
On foot, and floats, we're watching the PRIDE MARCH go blasting by
OTT colour-costumes, gold garish pomp and dizzying gender diversity
Whilst old-fart straights like me and the missus watch tearful, moved...

It began at 2 p.m. at The Walpole Bay Hotel in our own Cliftonville Rd.
Outs celebrating their freedom to be whatever the fuck they want
10 August 2019 supported by Kent groups like *Oasis* for domestic abuse
The *Sundowners Bar* and Staff, *Thanet Fire Engine* Crew, *Kent Police*
INLI Sea Rescue, Save Our NHS and Bollocks To Brexit bumper stickers...

Spice Girls' *Mel C* will play Dreamland tonight with Drag Queen band
Sink The Pink, both giving it some cockles and muscles

On the slope down Fort Road leading into the bay area and old town
We meet an elderly male gay couple, together 47 years, they're loving
The breeze-billowing riot of rainbow bunting and festooned balconies
Walls lined with wellwishers, pregnant women with stomachs painted
Families with little flags and complimentary whistles...

He's still as naughty now as he was then, one informs us, prodding
Laughing it off, but tearful at the progress made over the decades

Whitney Houston's "I Need Somebody To Love Me" is on Steel Drums
A magic-shoed Dorothy and her pals flank Mulan and two Dragons
The cross-dresser trans who serves us sticky buns in the Arcade waves
Rainbow coloured baths are pulled by Jolly Rogers and his ropes
Music is blasting from flats, Sink The Pink queen *Taylor Trash* showboats
Walking with *Asifa Lahore*, Britain's first publicly-out Muslim drag artist

Peter Tatchell, the legendary LGBTQ+ campaigner gives a speech
On the sea front stage by the parade to huge cheers and admiration
He walks of 67 countries worldwide still banning same sex relationships
Inflicting ancient prejudice with imprisonment, torture and even death
Including 37 that are part of the UK's Commonwealth

But us 60ts types, we just watch and smile, old enough to remember
The cruelty, the snide remarks, the stigma, the hatred and danger
And Dorothy, a long way from Kansas and her black & white bullyboys
Holds hands with Scarecrow and Tin Man, while Lion looks down at his
Heart, proudly open for all to see, beating loud, strong and true...

OUR NEW LIFE

Somewhere in the universe, a chrysalis opens
Letting loose all the colours within
Here, a mother cradles a scrunched up face
With a vanilla smell, the softest skin

As his parents look down in wonder and awe
At beauty that scorches their sky
Somewhere perfect, hope has burst into tears
And today, we now know why...

Tuesday, 8 September 2020
On the birth of their first child, a boy, MAXIMILLIAN (MAX)
To Alexandra Weber and Tom Coles
At Elizabeth The Queen Mother Hospital in Margate
Love from Mark, Mary Ann, Dean, Julia, Sean and all the family

RESILIENCE IN THE RAIN

Berenice Paolozzi was an Irish/Italian spiritual journeyman
Taken by Lymphoma in 2015, aged only forty-nine
I'd talked to her via Skype the year earlier about e-books
Helped enormously launching a wad load of mine

I've never forgotten that simple act of writer's generosity
We Irish chin-wagging like words might be banned
She'd become friends with my Mum and shared interests
In homeopathic cures, tapping into nature's hand

Berenice had been to India and studied empath abilities
In her search for an inner peace that whole sustains
But after five tenacious years of battling old procedures
It finally did for her; cancer gnawed away the reins

Reconciled with her daughter Nadia before the demise
They bedside-mended decades of familial division
Cremated in Ireland, but finally laid to rest on Italian soil
I see her bi-fold spirit revelling, a beautiful decision

Our time here is short and our pathways too precarious
And maybe it takes loss of life to remind us of such
But it's a miserable journey without compassion or love
The branch outstretched, positive people as crutch

I remember Berenice now as the beamer with panache
Rummaging in expression, question marking pain
She had an impish way about her, like one who giggles
At the breaks, embraces life, resilience in the rain...

For BERENICE PAOLOZZI who died 6 June 2015
A Friend of my Mum and the Family in Clontarf, Dublin
Her daughter is Nadia Forde, Celebrated Irish Model and Singer

AWKWARD REACH

On the lurid surface, Britney Spears is just another wastrel Popster
Who doesn't warrant such ludicrous publicity or care?
But on closer examination of her totally controlled incarceration
We find manipulative Daddykins, working her despair

But a movement got going, holding up message-word placards
Have been working the public's short span of attention
Screaming like hurt children for Spear's legalese conservatorship
To end after 14 years of enforced controlled detention

But I wonder why such a waspy girly singer and her car crash life
Should elicit such a frenzied public outpour of emotion?
Clutching their radios in awe as she testifies in a macho US court
Her crew shivering in total allegiance and fan devotion

Is it that deep down inside all of us, lurks the secret terror thought
That we too are subjected to a reign of controlling ties?
Are we all just well trained easy-to-shape lemmings marching to
Jackboots; to someone else's cleverly constructed lies?

Having power over your personal life, choices, finances and kids
And to monetize it, is a legally horrific freedom breach
So I wish the lady singer fresh growing up years with her children
And God Bless *All Protestors* and their *Awkward Reach*...

For BRITNEY SPEARS and her carers

CARACTACUS POTTS GETS LAID

I was transported to the precipice of a plunge waterfall
That stunning crescendo of mist and abandon below
I can remember your contours like electrical conductors
Steering me to places where only the lucky get to go

It wasn't my first arc-rainbow, but it was my first with you
After months of dancing around a slow inner flame
We both knew it would change our former party soirees
Redefine that mutually beneficial friendship game

There had been pointers to our Universal enlightenment
Capped by fears of stepping onto mines too soon
Caractacus Potts off to India on his Maharaja adventure
Wooing the winds of love in his sentry-box balloon

All these decades have passed and it's still luminescent
The calm in that bedroom after our first deep dive
Where the past receded and there was only the future
With brand new coordinates, all tingling and alive...

DAD I'M IN REHEARSALS

Our youngest Sean left home when he was eighteen
And in general, hasn't been seen since
When he does call, it's monosyllabic grunt-responses
And a feeling that his hair needs a rinse

But I couldn't be more proud of our hipster go-getter
Chasing his dream, storming the breach
Father-to-Son ratio, I wonder which one of us will be
The L-Plate burner with wisdom to teach

Bought him a £20 electric guitar in the Salvation Army
Built his own PC at thirteen from scratch
Looks like David Bowie and writes songs that emulate
Was in a band, gone solo, future catch

There's a whole world out there to experience-savour
Places to go and wondrous sights to see
Hopefully we will have passed on an emotional atlas
To deal with life's heartache/complexity

Success is a lottery of talent, graft and savvy choices
The doors leading topside, skinny and thin
So when I hear their mantra, "Dad I'm In Rehearsals"
I'm thinking one of us might actually get in

If you don't take the chances, twist instead of a stick
You'll be one of those perpetual *'what ifs'*
So good luck and bon voyage our beautiful gambler
Ride your bicycle right off rejection's cliffs...

For our son SEAN/FRANCIS

HAND TOWELS FOR PONTIUS PILATE
(An Unholy Mess)

Good Quintus, Take a letter to Augustus; date 1BC RSVP PDQ
Because I dreamt of Caesar and The Ides of March
Also mention I've had Hellish problems with my toga laundries
Probably vinegar mixed in with their Christian starch

You've probably seen my previous requests for 20 hand towels
And enclosed are pieces of silver to match that fee
You see, ever since I absolved myself of that Galilean prophet
They seem to pass on every *I'm God* agitator to me

Gussie baby, I came to Judaea to seek Roman fame/fortune
Maybe trade with Pharisee crooks, sleep with slaves
But all I get to do is sentence to crucifixion braggers like Jesus
Who now says he'll soon be sauntering out of graves

And credit where it's due, apparently he's doing big miracles
On lepers, whores and other marginal taxation bands
But I must confess Gaius, that although I scrub with oil all night
I can't seem to purge this reddish hue inking my hands

So if you can stop mosaic-making and eating grapes for a mo
Please send fresh linen to the enclosed Jew address
Because I swear to the almighty Zeus, I've rubbed my skin raw
And can't seem to rinse out this stain; this *unholy mess*...

FLAT PACK APPEAL

I recently started dating a KNOXHULT flat-pack kitchen from IKEA
And despite our cultural differences, it worked surprisingly well
But then I caught her eyeing up a machismo hardwood Spatula
Leering saucily over by the sustainably sourced Cranberry gel

Love is a harsh mistress, sleeping with minimalist anthracite is worse
As I sat violated in their scrupulously clean Scandinavian bog
Of course I should have seen the signs of their matte finish infidelity
When I saw her saucily stroking his thick and manly catalogue

She stood there in her professionally installed scratchproof reversal
As if her dual-purpose sink taps were not a phallic temptation
While I licked my wounds with 16-meatballs and 8 Juice Cleansers
Cursing the Lord of all Scandi Home Improvement installation

So if you're tempted to have an affair with a curvaceous base unit
And hope that her declarations of a lifetime guarantee is real
Remember to keep a Hawkeye out for utensils and well-hard Woks
Trying to lure your lady away with their Swedish Stainless Steel...

KEEPERS OF THE GATES (Endangered Species)

Secondhand Book Shops are disappearing everywhere
Unable to make real-world logistics work

Emporiums of the Past, Present and Future
They're the most magical places on earth to me (always have been)
Filled with mind-blowing and mind-expanding amounts of treasure
Gunnel-high with goodies, the custodians of Storyville
That thrilled once and will ignite mind-quivers again
And I've longed to travel to the world's quirkiest page-turning bazaars
Tell A Story uses a Portuguese van, *Singing Wind*, an Arizona cattle farm
Half-a-mile of stores/book-publishers are on *College Street* in Calcutta
Alta Acqua Libreria is on a gondola in Venice (my missus has been)

Undoubtedly cheaper and more accessible by hopper bus
Personally, I prefer *Pilgrim's Hospice* in Margate's Old Town Parade
A classic two-floored corner UK building that was once a Midlands Bank
(Like *Munro's Books in Victoria*, Canada, complete with vaults)
But now serves a higher and more dignified purpose
Keeping my ilk supplied with rare autobiographies, ordnance survey maps
Latest eclectic fiction, local poetry, history, military and sports tomes
A children's corner for all the DFL moms; upstairs for the Arts and Paintings
All bag-buddied with DVD, BLU RAY Box Sets and Limited Edition CDs...

Book people are a weird bunch; all the manic tingle of vinyl collectors
With just as much philistine-destroy inner-burn should you incorrectly
Reference something clearly out of your mental depth

But like so much of what we love and still want to treasure
Keepers of the Gates are becoming an endangered species
In a world where intangible online abundance is described as a win
And Yes, I use Net giants like everyone else for their price and speed post
But I pine, more and more, for the surprise, the discoveries and rewards
And only when we were culled of freedom (like in pandemic lockdown)
Denied a simple browse; did we finally understand such value and loss

A great book taps into reflections of other worlds that become ours
Their ideas sparking thought, creativity, even inspired bravado choices

Book piles are like medicine vials, roadmaps and companions, pointers
A gateway into warm for us that need the feel and smell of turning pages
To make tangible, what we can only dare to dream...

CREAMY ACQUISITIONS

Surgeon Dick Ever Hard, a close relative of Dr. Hardwick
Is helping Nurse DD overcome her fear of pleasure
He's lubricating her mountainous Kim Kardashian assets
With his truncheon of some considerable measure

Johnny Deep Dong, the unhygienic Pirate of Jizney Land
Is making sure that his Ample Amber can be heard
While Gobble Hood and Friar Sucks of Batty Man's Forest
Both show Maid Marion how to share a Royal Laird

Princess Areola of Tit Two-Teen is showering in the Falcon
But is soon joined by Schlong Solo in the all together
They get jiggy with the heavy breathing of a threesome
Feeling the Force of Girth Vadar's Imperial Leather

William Master Bates is reading poetry to Anastasia Anal
Treading not so softly on her bolt upright posterior
He later climaxes and she gains his hot rhyming couplets
Enjoying his creamy acquisitions, inside & exterior

So spare a thought for Sherlock Bones at 38GG Baker St.
Handling his biggest ever case of Baskerville Bush
Say a prayer for Matron Mammaries of The Big 'O' Clinic
Who caught Brandon Iron's bird-watching thrush

Lord, help YouTube secretaries and their sticky workloads
Dressed in tight skirts with four blouse buttons loose
And thank God for Betty Baps, who just saved the planet
Cleverly handed her boss tissues, for *ecological use*...

A QUESTION OF WHEN

Salman Rushdie is on the television again
Hunted for writing a book
Gross-out intransigents hounding him
With their sickening religious bile

How great then dear was my colossal sin
That you were *so taken aback*
Did your family's crib-sheet out-do mine
In their shit-for-brains comment count

How about the worthy letter you proffered
The things you said to friends
Who are now, of course, entirely convinced
That they *used* to know me, used to...

This means war...
Cry havoc and let loose the dogs...
Hell hath no fury...
I'm literally living all of the fucking clichés

What am I looking for?
Why do I need *you* to make *me* worthy?
Who has the power to solve this?
The sweet grace to forgive

We used to work together once
We toughed it out before this, you and I
But you raised so much more than your voice
That vicious day, and I more than race

Another TV program shows a glass box
With a coiled snake and a titmouse
The titmouse dodges and parries
As the shadow of the serpent rises up

Incapable of leniency now
The monster hisses before it strikes
It's not a question of how
It's just a question of when...

BIG CHEESE COMES A CROPPER

Limburger, Schloss, Raclette, Livarot and Camembert
Are some of the world's more pungent cheeses
Many foodies get sexually aroused at a saucy wench
Beneath a dairy cow doing rapid titty squeezes

But if I actually tooth into veined Gorgonzola or Stilton
Salivating over its pimply rind with lactic desires
I can't help thinking that all this locally sourced mould
Tastes like a set of backend balding Pirelli tyres

I'll stick to a Mascarpone and Wallace's Wensleydale
Melting softly on the tongue, flavoursome both
And avoid those myriad fancy-pants artisan creations
All stinky on the hooter and chalk on the throat...

PROLONGED EXPOSURE TO PROTESTANTS (Religiosity Part 1)

They can't help themselves I suppose and one wants to be nice
But we Catholics like a bit of blood curdling inquisition
None of your half-assed weedy Presbyterian jolly nice chappies
We want flagellation and other such acts of contrition

And for the love of God don't get me started on your Protestant
Who thinks Henry The VIII was too lenient with his wives
We like a sexy witch boiled in cooking oil on a nice steady flame
Professing her love for Satan and coming out in hives

If a man isn't being crucified or tortured in manacles for Venial Sin
We feel unloved, like a BBC Jimmy Saville blow-up doll
If there isn't pain and suffering and unrelenting fire and brimstone
We're like Oswald without a scope on the grassy knoll

But I take comfort in a God of Mercy who will forgive Protestants
When they join the *misguided* queue at the Pearly Gates
Catholic Priests singing four-part harmonies about rampant gays
Selling world-class eternal penance at discounted rates

I'm spreading my love of Jesus & white people and Republicans
By filing Donald Trump's *Humanitarian of the Year* report
On his knees at the altar of Stormy Daniel's Pole Dancing Benefit
Staring up at her considerably huge double-digit support

I myself have sent in my application for sainthood to the Vatican
Typed on lurid pink headed-paper by the Pet Shop Boys
But they're fierce sluggish in the Department of Halo Nomination
Probably shouldn't have included phallic operated toys?

So I'm off now to again avoid *Prolonged Exposure to Protestants*
Over a spot of cat-of-nine-tails blood and eyeballs lunch
And thank the Good Lord I'm a masochistic bloodthirsty Catholic
Blessed with the biggest fucked-up beliefs of the bunch...

PUNCHING OUT CATHOLICS (Religiosity Part 2)

Myself and the better half are hoping for grandchildren
But our spawn is so *slow* off the procreational spot
They can't seem to decide whether to gun for progeny
Or forgo this whole-life-commitment thingy as grot

The thrill of changing shitty nappies and screaming tots
Wiggling in buggy strollers no soother can placate
Should be on us like a soggy-bottom rash for Sudocrem
Mothercare pram-spirals dangling, all eco-ornate

But one can hope and dream, that they'll soon spread
Joy and mirth, even if it isn't their legs and sperm
While we wait for onesies to be dragged out of storage
And look up fees of crèches; dates for half term

We wish them love and happiness and healthy lifestyles
Free from office stress and money worries galore
It's just that when it comes to serious parental fretfulness
We'd quite like to be stressed a fuck-load more...

REOPENING PURGATORY (Religiosity Part 3)

In a staggeringly inconvenient dictate by The Catholic Church
They've closed down *Purgatory* for all transitioning sinners
Now you're shoved onto the Flaming 'H' Express Train to Hades
No sly shortcuts for baddies acting like penitent beginners

I had hoped to do a hundred years here or a millennium there
And ease my Soul away from the bummer of damnation
But now I have to be nice and saintly absolutely all of the time
If I'm to avoid an eternity of TV Soaps and SS flagellation

Apparently the Lord of the Underworld is thrilled at the decision
It means he can get Souls quicker onto retribution's ropes
You'll be hobnobbing with gutless politicians who didn't protect
Women and children; chit-chat with 13 duplicitous Popes

Sometimes I ask how rapists and kiddy-fiddlers all escape justice
Why don't our elected officials actually update old laws?
Maybe it was those duplicitous cunts that mothballed Purgatory
Because a perpetrator always has an innocent in its jaws

Heaven is a place we want to exist and *God Is Bounteous Love*
But the reality of life is many horror-merchants never pay
Maybe that's why the *One True Church* and its legal appeasers
Want control over what constitutes your redemption day

I have to believe that the righteous and the kind and the good
Live on in a better plain than this cheapass compromise
And when I pass away, the ones who fought for us will greet me
Not cold lawyers with interpretive out-clauses in their eyes...

DAVID ATTENBOROUGH'S EGG TIMER

On a wall-mounted angle-pivoting 4K Samsung 75-inch tele in Hades
(The preferred choice always)
Lucifer screens a mural that's he's spotted during routine surveillance
Of the one world he most desperately wants to reduce to dust
Expertly painted on a Lido wall in Margate...

Interestingly, the street artist has used the side of an entire building
(Days of work on aluminium scaffolding with seriously old boards)
And it's a shockingly professional portrait
Of the world-renowned elderly environmentalist
David Attenborough
Holding a running-out-of-time egg timer in one hand
And a plastic bottle of mineral water in the other...

The product name is cleverly changed from Evian to Naïve
And beside it are comments about plastic eventually replacing
All fish as the dominant substance in the sea by the year 2050

But Lucifer's interest lies in another can-spraying Pollock-come-Pillock
Already grabbing back the bottom half of the beautifully realised wall
Regardless of its stunning nature and smarts

Then another gets greedy too...
And once started, given reign by the first, and in only a matter of days
All but the upper face of the visionary crusader is showing
The rest of him obliterated by ego
And incomprehensible gold and pink squiggly letters...

Lucifer licks his lips in glee
This is how he likes it - slow - steady - creeping
A pertinent and timely message in a work of art – wiped by ego
Like an entire species or children snuffed out in wars

The truth suffocating beneath garish noise and bluster
And the surface future generations will need - literally being defaced

And when the crusader is no longer be with us, timer drained
Darkness will exit its throne to survey a sea of swill
An oily layer of our not so clever shit...relishing the salty tears of fools...

For DAVID ATTENBOROUGH and Environmentalists

THE BLESSED EDDIE

We take things for granted in the access-all-areas Internet Age
Get blasé about innovators, the game-changers for real
I can remember when *Eddie Van Halen* first happened in Rock
Most guitar-players dropped down to genuflect & kneel

I wrote lyrics for a band in Dublin, called him *The Blessed Eddie*
And we worshipped at the altar of those first two WB LPs
Our jaw dropped to the floor at the cool riffs and hammer-ons
A staggering musicality beneath his technical expertise

By the time they got to album number six and flash MTV videos
Van Halen was one of the famous axemen anywhere
A solo flourish in the magical *Back To The Future* movie in 1985
Cemented his legend, but also brought fame despair

Citing inevitable differences, he left his Dutch namesake band
As his physical health deteriorated & medicines failed
But when he passed Oct 2020 from cancer, and aged only 65
Millions were genuinely destroyed, his genius derailed

But I always return to *Panama*, *Little Guitars* & *Hot For Teacher*
To get my shot of pyrotechnics and hairy Eighties fun
And smile like a teen with a brand new chew toy called *God*
When I listen to The Blessed Eddie prove, he was <u>one</u>....

For EDDIE VAN HALEN ad all our Guitar Heroes

FIXED BAYONETS

Chain smoking and finger tapping on our Formica kitchen table
You told me sheepishly what you'd discovered about yourself
As far back as a year ago...

You half-laughed. It's not been easy. It's not been peachy man
Always known down deep, yet oddly hard to wrap around/accept
You sighed like a hundred-year old woman aching for peace
The winding Yellow Brick Road had answers at least, at the end...

What could I say? How could I help? What could I even do?
What offerings of mental magic could I produce in situ?
Awkwardly passing off your emotional Hell as a phase
A temporary leaning due to chronic loneliness, a Limbo of sorts...

I tried to be understanding and kind; that was the best thing to do
Be open, listen closely, thinking quick of ashtrays for your ashes
A cradle for all those incinerated tears and scorches to come

The other girls were being great about it really, supportive
Yet I could see how exposed and vulnerable you'd become
Society fortresses now barefaced for all to stone and arrow
Everything that was sheer and certain, now jagged and raw...

Would your friends really stay friends? Your parents completely flip?
Turn dictionary-dogs on the black sheep, the gender deviant
Apply dictatorial erasers, neat in their methods, no muss, no fuss,
No mascaraed diamond dogs living amongst the likes of us...

You lunged at the empty ciggy twenty-carton on my kitchen table
Crumpling your physical crutch with a suddenly violent hand
"...There's plenty more where they came from..." you barked
As if being angry with someone would help

Then with a genuine thank-you nod and a huge lung-intake sigh
You added a stoical smile, head up regardless, fixed bayonets

As you walked out the door into a new future
Of shape-shifting plumes
And different-tasting cigarettes...

VIRGIN VS 181

Six hundred and fifty British politicians suddenly went to stupid school
When it came to public taxation being judiciously allocated
They gave estimates of 300 + million for the re-model of two palaces
Because they knew those low sums, kept outrage placated

So the sycophantic BBC/Press craftily avoided any final-bill discussion
About the real-world hardships of three point one billion awry
You can't have the truth on the British Airwaves making punters think
When you're fucking over their loved ones with a shameful lie

Licking the arse of British Royalty has corrupted UK journalism for eons
Because lucrative photos help sell all of those colluding rags
So "God Save The Queen" by The Sex Pistols on Virgin Records VS 181
Highlighting indoctrination, has way too many message flags

British Establishment pissed their collective knighthoods, raged against
Such gobby insolence, questioning their lucrative gravy train
Too aggressive, too disrespectful and voters should know their betters
Are the excuses peddled, their rehearsed diversionary refrain

People should ask why VS 181's excommunicated from public playlists
Or why the withdrawn A&M-original now sells for such dosh?
Because this song was the last great stand of combative individualism
Before we sappy succumbed to compliancy, the easy kosh

I don't know how many succubae are on the secretive Royal Civil List
Or the hidden holocaust attributed to their sly billions skiving
But I know common folk won our freedom with gutsy fighter courage
And not the privileged Edward, his hands-on Nazi conniving

So you can stick your curtsy protocol and subserviently bowing down
Bollocks to Royalist indoctrination, a sheep-like "God Save..."
Because I will always see UK Politicians swindling our children's future
As the real moronic consequence of their benevolent wave...

For THE SEX PISTOLS, PUNK ROCK and all the NEW WAVERS

BOO BOO
(All That Ever Made Sense)

Dust-jacket inscriptions declaring our undying love
Weigh down shelves in our local recycle store
Initials carved into trees and lank electricity pylons
Arrow-hearts accompany every garage door

Personalized birthday messages gush about years
And how age has gone in the wrong direction
It's as if the sheer cost of this intellectual purchase
Dutifully mirrors the senders depth of affection

But are all those promises of devotion still as strong
Or has time worn down their potency to blur
He may no longer rock Capt. Chisel-Jaw Coolsville
She may have to concede and jowl concur

I'm thinking of a friend we phoned on Wednesday
But was gone by Saturday's cardiac attack
Michael who adored Delta Blues and Rock 'n' Roll
Collected his heroes in yellowed paperback

His Little Richard bio sported a blue biro dedication
A March 85 birthday gift from his adoring gal
Boo Boo describes herself as a self-deprecating twit
Lucky to have found her such a similar-ish pal

The sheer commerce of life has us discarding things
We once saw as too precious to give away
But compassion recycles itself into all ongoing need
Someone else soaking up inspiration today

Our jacket-posts may seem passé-lore to future gen
Casually browsing declarations once intense
But even if they're faded now and reduced for sale
They're still love and all that ever made sense...

For MICHAEL and MARILYN ABRAMOV

CHALK ON SEA WALLS

Here we are, in our suburban-sensible clothes and sturdy shoes
Drawing like giddy schoolkids on the Sea Wall of Joss Bay
Lapping up the Margate air and the tentative April sunshine
Collecting fossils and husks on a sheltered coastal beach...

In a moment of male transcendental genius and Zen wisdom
I stand Monet-like with my seaside-pencil and scrawl *Steely Dan*
You on the other hand, start an elaborate white-chalk-mural
The canvas of which is six-times the size of mine and growing

Alert and smiling; it's a side-profile of a young woman's face
Her bug eyes are staring forward, but her huge mane of hair
Stretches back and down over six evenly-spaced wavy-lines
Making the image look 70ts-cool and happening hippy-chick

We moved down from London's big choke to a breezy town
Away from the hospitals and cancer and the quad bi-passes
And the puking and the tablets and the endless blood tests
Free to wander beaches and fields and breathe in fresh air
Take on a new life, a new chapter and Chalk On Sea Walls...

We iPhone our Banksy moments with an up-message to Dino
Our special-needs son who also loves the wind and the sea
Then FaceBook-share our Mark and Mary Ann *Vision On* Art
With friends and two other beloved coup-flown siblings...

Bodily-battered, bruised and still getting our brain bearings
You're 60 on the 20th of April 2018 – me on September 28th
Are we young? Are we old? Are we somewhere in-between?
Who are those bods reflected in the shop pane as we pass?
Life is so brief, washed away in seconds, make your mark or...

But then I see you – soft shoes off – toes scrunching the sand
Going at the wall with lady-gusto and the tingle of creation

Drawing line after wavy line, her energy-hair stretching back
Across 30-years, while her white-blue eyes look ever forward
Confident, full of beans, chi flowing through those sexy locks
Hopeful, impossibly cute, lovely – and so glad to be alive...

A FAILED PYROMANIAC CURSES ANTS

The symmetrical beauty of a fat box of Swan Matches
Followed by the yellow orgasm of bursting flame
Ever since I stopped being Teenage Mark Pyromaniac
My flamin' life has never been the flamin' same

When we were kids, we just wanted to set fire to stuff
Post-box slits and neighbour's creosoted fences
Any chance to blow shit up with two copper bombs
Felt like a Sherbet Fountain sizzlers on the senses

We bought cap guns, sparklers and boxes of bangers
Emulating gunpowder nutters of Historical yore
When we'd finished terrifying strays and shopkeepers
We'd leg it to Moore St. and buy us some more

But my path as a manically giggling Mozart-ish arsonist
Was cruelly stopped by a conscience one day
While I was frying a Dublin ant with a magnifying glass
I got soppy and let the squirt skedaddle away

Now the smell of sulphur is limited to our wood-burner
And Paraffin to soaked white-firelighter-squares
I long for the simplicity of torching municipal buildings
Singeing my newly minted tussock of pubic hairs

But alas my would-be life of *Sergeant Major Firestarter*
Has evaporated like a cigarette packet warning
But there's still days when I hunker shirtless by my Huey
And dream of Napalm, *so fragrant* in the morning...

BOB HOPE IN THE KNACKER'S YARD

Famously waspish, Betty Davis once cackled, *getting old is not for sissies*
Clive James chiselled out more honest poetry in his Cancer's demise
Jenny Joseph demanded that we wear purple and red in our dotage
Two-finger the curtain-peepers with mad colours that bleed the eyes

Bob Monkhouse catalogued one million laughs in his meticulous diaries
Even when he himself was often considered to be a bit of a joke
Winston Churchill was said to be permanently sozzled towards the end
As he painted his daughter's loss amidst clouds of Cuban smoke

Mahatma Gandhi advised us to live each day as if you'll die tomorrow
Mohammed Ali had an interfaith funeral to heal centuries of scars
The Hollies sang of The Air That I Breathe and only needing to love you
Oscar Wilde warned of gutters and to try to live amongst the stars

Just shy of the knacker's yard, I sit with a hernia-distended belly button
And lengthy open-heart surgery lines on my chest and both my legs
Between the wheezing, farting and the discreetly elasticated waistline
I tend to forests of nasal hair and jammies that whiff of urinary dregs

Yuck pass-remarkable, Bob Hope is hosting the 1970 Miss World Contest
Asking questions of babes in bikinis that would horrify top misogynists
In 2022, there's a supposed art exhibition at the Margate Turner Gallery
That would make the Emperor in New Clothes slash his conman wrists

How do we stay true to ourselves, if at the end we're still evading truth?
As we laugh and point at our television sets at those dropping the ball
Am I Stalin signing 5000 death certificates late in the Communist night?
A horse killer stirring a vat of glue, uniform rifle squad aimed at a wall?

Adolf Hitler said nothing of any value and was burned after his suicide
Mosley's black-shirt fascism lay crushed by the English working class
J.R.R. Tolkien fired the breathtaking imagination of whole generations
Defeated Mordor evil through Gandalf's battle cry, *you shall not pass*

When it comes to my deathbed close up and Cecil B. DeMille says cut
Will I meekly ask for another go round, attempt a deeper better take?
Or will I bow out classy like Grace and Frankie in dignified acceptance
Glad that I was here, and with loved ones, still trying for trying's sake...

LICKING STICK
(The Promised Land and Its Borders)

Svelte Jennifer Fitzgerald had the most fantastic rack
Near her ample blouse, we could barely speak
And as she sashayed across the yard working her lolly
Our collective legs went full-bore jellyfish weak

But other sections of our burgeoning anatomies stirred
As she jiggled with her mates and so did they
She'd stare across at clusters of uniformed teen cuties
Licking that stick in her decidedly phallic way

It's rumoured she took Jockser Molloy behind the shed
Where she raised more than his IQ and hope
He confirmed that wonders lay in Jenny's fitted cotton
And that both hands were needed to cope

Jenny was an Air Hostess in Executive Class, last I heard
Serving businessmen with peanuts and a drink
Leaning into their sightline with luxury accommodations
Exiting with a husband unable to rational think

I often dote on her persuasive miracles in adult dreams
And smile at those deliberate lollipop strokes
Grin at a woman who whipped us newbees into shape
Made men out of twerps and pitiable blokes

I imagine Jen still turns heads when she walks into a pub
The barman suddenly inundated with orders
Make mine a double mate, because God is bounteous
He's sent *The Promised Land 'and' its Borders...*

DELICIOUS ALOYSIUS

When I was 10 years old and still in short pants, pre colour-tele
I was obsessed with *Gerry Anderson's Thunderbirds*

Never more so than with the interchangeable piston-pushed
Upload pods in Virgil's flying workhorse *Thunderbirds 2*

Contained within these phantasmagorical brown domes
Sat an array of innovational rescue kit, FAB Electrical Elastoplasts
For every falling skyscraper, sinking chemical ship, pit of peril
Collapsing suspension bridge and burning telecoms tower

Also in there was the bright yellow underwater craft *Thunderbirds 4*
Piloted by Gordon Tracy, aquanaut and all round good egg
Scott Tracy commanding his troops in the superfast *Thunderbirds 1*
And if you ever needed to fix the wayward trajectory of a Sun Probe
Alan Tracy would travail black outer space in the red *Thunderbird 3*

On lonely duty up in orbit, John Tracy maintained *Thunderbird 5*
Listening to global broadcasts, pleas for help in hopeless scenarios
Reporting back to the wise Jeff Tracy, father and reclusive millionaire
On *Tracy Island*, their closely guarded secret oceanic IR base
(I'm 10, I won't tell boys, I Pinky promise)
And all of *International Rescue* especially designed by Brains
Their "Uh, uh, Yes Mr. Tracy..." resident inventor and dotty genius...

Always-immaculate pre mission, Scott and Virgil's little blue uniforms
Would end every episode tattered and torn post intervention
Their flushed wooden faces covered in Vaseline and dirt smudges
Bookended by *Thunderbirds Are Go!* Barry Gray's stunning theme
A bandstand march that still moves the blood and waters the eyes

But of all the thrills in this imagined 2060s Supermarionation TV Show
None beat David Graham, a Veteran British actor/voice-over giant
Who gave his brilliance to five huge screen characters in the show...
Gordon Tracy, the aquanaut for Thunderbirds 4
Kyrano, father of Tin-Tin and Brains
Visionary scientist and engineer (and his talking robot Braman)

But most famous of all was the proper Cockney Butler
And uniformed Chauffeur to the posh London Agent Lady Penelope
The mighty done-some-porridge *Aloysius "Nosey" Parker*
Or just *Parker* as we schoolkids in tele-land knew him

I may have envied their life-sized photos on the lounge-room wall
Flipping up and backwards into secret tunnels for uniform changing
Then sat on sofas moving along transport rails to huge parked rockets
That counted down and blasted off out of a parting swimming pool
It's palm tree wobbling as the jet fumes passed (well of course it did)
I may even have fancied Lady Penelope voiced by Sylvia Anderson
(Gerry Anderson's wife) with her slinky uppercrust sexpot tones...

But none assuaged my fandom of the loveable rogue that was *Parker*
Delicious Aloysius, shifty-fingered and nimble of banter
Friend of Diamond Dave from Dagenham
Who knew people and how to acquire things
Who in turn could talk to Lopsided George
Down at The Gas & Gaiters come Friday lunchtime (sweet as)...

Parker, blasting away the gates of some evil corporation
With the guns of his employer's long pink Rolls Royce
Her Browning equalisers hidden in the sleek beast's front headlights
Like a female James Bond, way ahead of her time

Parker, the cheeky chappy
Master of all trades both legal and questionable
The how's-your-father sure-fire bet for the three-thirty at Cheltenham
The voice of a talented Englishman I didn't know defining my youth
Maybe even my love of English girls

Jowl-cheeked *Parker*
An old-school villain given the combination to a second-chance safe
That would not lead to porridge and lumpy pillows

But this time, because of his good lady's trust
A former wrong-un now sits at the wheel, all guns blazing

Delicious Aloysius Parker
Happy to be doing right by the little guy for his bit of proper posh...

For GERRY ANDERSON and his fantastic creations and crew

NATURE'S LED ZEPPELIN
(Drunk Bumble Bee)

The Led Zeppelin of the insect world is the Bumble Bee
Constantly pissed, lecherous, boogies all night
This unlikely Rock 'n' Roller may look all colours cuddly
But he can pollinate every ripe tomato in sight

Nature's lead singer gets drunk on excess nectar shots
Then shags every female with his petal power
When he's had his wicked way and is pollen-jizz spent
Percy then conks out in someone else's flower

In every garden tended everywhere on this old planet
Flower Beds, Vegetables, Shrubberies abound
Sometimes water running, catch butterflies tag scents
The soft hum of Nature, its rejuvenation sound

It's said that if the bees die, then humanity's next to go
And isn't it ironic that our fate is on some drunk
A huge Bumble Bee got stuck behind our kitchen door
Go you beauty, Stairway To Heaven your spunk....

For AILEEN, KELLY, ANGELA, TED and JARRED and LORNA
In Cliftonville's Clarendon Road, Margate
And for MARY ANN, CATHERINE and JONATHAN
Our Constant Gardeners, one and all

FLICKING SHEETS

This is how life is
The stuff of it
Moments that define us
Pick-me-ups for the weary heart

I'm making a pull out bed with our two year-old Daughter
Flicking a base sheet over the bare mattress
I hold it in the air for a few seconds
And it hovers

In awe
She watches it flap and fly
Her tiny gobsmacked jaw
Comically plonked on the floorboard below
Her entire being enrapt at such a wondrous thing

All brand new and giggly-brilliant
She shouts out, "Do it again Daddy!"
So I give it some serious Peter Pan

And as if possessed of magical properties
Mummy's Miracle Persil Canvas
Shimmers and sails and air-dances
Before settling down gently once more on the bed
In a bear-hug for the whole wide world

As adults we wouldn't think of it as something special
It's a mundane thing really
Everyday stuff
Flicking sheets

But to her child's eyes
It's unutterably fantastic
Possibility, Wonder and Promise

Memory-chest beautiful
Like Julia Hope, aged 2

For our JULIA HOPE

MARTYRED FOREVER
(Chide Abide)

Like the next man, I admire a person with spunk and mettle
Willing to go ten rounds with doubt, proper bellicose
But there's another part of me knows that unless you curve
Fill relationships with compromise; loneliness is close

You've got to chide abide, take the taunts and slag drags
Though seething with rage, will yourself to *mediate*
Keep the flame alive by middle-ground/accommodating
Longevity and happiness require a lot of sublimate

We sling grappling hooks on the ramparts of relationships
Making our dictatorial and emotionally rigid stand
Vow to surrender no further love to this latest soul partner
Stomp off into alone, leading your marching band

Stuck in your craw, can't be the real deal, sold out myself
All these textbook thoughts cajole and sucker clever
But there is no one who hasn't thrown the first angry stone
And wished its ripple effect hadn't *martyred forever...*

KIDS

In Dublin's Drimnagh
Walking down the silent volcano of
Benbulbin Road

Where blue and white statues of the Immaculate Heart of Mary
Quietly stand guard in doorway arches
Seeing off poxbottles and shysters and gobshites...

Through the deaf of you gone, Bernie
I hear the beautiful sound of children

School kids...
Screamin' and shoutin' at the top of their voices
As they mill round the rain-smooth feet-worn concrete
Throwing chewed-up biros at Jockser Doyle's egghead
And big-mouth Slattery sticking Golfball chewing-gum
Into his pencil box on the sly as fatso O'Toole scoffs down Aniseed Balls
And Joyces of Cork Raspberry bars and farty-pants Decko
Goes all puffer fish in the left cheek as the mopey eejet
Tries to break down an Everlasting Gobstopper with a teeny jaw...

School kids...
Like an unstoppable torrent
Careering across the schoolyard
Swallowing up the World

I know how you loved those kids Bernie, I know
The tears that would well up in your eyes
When their loveliness touched you
And you'd reach out and hug me
Excited for the future...

Let's go over and talk to them, Bernie
You and I, let's go over and talk to them
And glow in their warmth
And wallow and bathe
In the lovely laughter of living...

For BERNADETTE O'DONNELL killed 3 May 1980
In a car-accident in Wicklow, Ireland, while youth hostelling
With all my love and affection - her one-time boyfriend

ONE OUT OF SIX

Mr. Loughlan was our Science Teacher in O'Connell's School
And when the leather came out, he hit you only once
He was probably six three and as that palm stroke registered
You quickly avowed to no longer be classroom dunce

The Christian Brothers and Unchristian Sisters relished the lash
And more than a few sadists stood in their unholy ranks
But they nailed the highest grades in Dublin and Nationwide
And despite some wavering, most parents gave thanks

But while discipline was necessary to control hormonal teens
The barbarity of ruler/caners too often got out of hand
As the Seventies morphed into the more enlightened Eighties
Corporal Punishment wasn't mellowed; it was banned

Loughlan was respected and in his class no one took the piss
He didn't leather often but was feared enough to avoid
And I recall, his teacher's bint was get results, use as weapon
He turned out fighters, and not another placating droid

The spare-the-rod argument has raged on for decades since
Has a past six-of-the-best created fuel for future violence
Yet look at how academically useless Education has become
I wonder if a firm hand, wasn't just driven common sense

In a fairer society, where soft children's gentility is celebrated
We needn't worry about every haunted face in school
But the truth is that without the emotional armour of achieve
Our kids are just a new form of lame; an ill equipped fool...

I'VE NEVER SLEPT WITH HARVEY WEINSTEIN
THOUGH GOD KNOWS I'VE TRIED
(In the Dock with a Hollywood A-Lister)

When I stepped out of the lift your honour, it was two a.m.
And Harvey was in a bathrobe, inviting me inside
I thought it was about a part in a life-changing film project
Acknowledge my talents with his big manly pride

When he assured me that this *was* the auditioning process
I remembered my friends said, fealty seals the deal
I'd heard of Hollywood hypocrisy amongst moguls for sure
But I was young, and his interest in me seemed real

So I came along this afternoon your honour to help clarify
Be at one with my wronged co-workers in 'MeToo'
Yes there's a crew recording my admirable benevolence
A hairdresser, lifestyle coach and Vegetarian Guru

Sat at home during the worldwide pandemic your honour
I took a year off to read scripts, latte denial crazed
I knew that none of the bigger interviewers or TV channels
Would question my nurse betrayal, $$s never raised

You see they love me no matter what! I couldn't care less!
I can literally get away with murder! They appease!
It's repeated in England, Europe, Asia, Japan and Australia
Won't rock the boat with ratings, nor fame displease

But regarding Harvey Weinstein your honour, I must divulge
I heard nothing for years about his sickening dupes
It was someone else's fault you see and we remain chaste
That's the line given by all the rich and famous troops

Years later, I was on the red carpet in a revealing plunger
I didn't mind standing by him when statues lay within
"I've never slept with Harvey Weinstein your honour, oh no
I'm just here researching a role, *one I deserve to win...*"

VAMPIRE ISN'T CONCERNED

In the late 19th century, I was walking the streets of Budapest
When I picked up on a new aroma, icky and strange
It wasn't the usual crew of scrawny unwashed Euro peasants
Wafting out of the brothels and taverns, down range

Admittedly in need of a late dinner, I was tucking into a neck
When this clinically morbid fat fucker sauntered past
He was all dandified and quaffs and quills and puffy perfume
Dropped my serving-wench aperitif pretty damn fast

I've learned from experience to sniff out dirty arterial cancer
A bouquet of corpuscles I find most unpalatable, foul
And as diet has improved with agricultural over-productivity
I no longer need to raise my cloak, hypnotize or howl

As the centuries have passed and humanity has grown obese
It's no longer gentry who fill my blood lust with a chill
You're all so fucking huge; I just do the bat over a McDonalds
And I find a proportional porker to vein-drain and kill

There was a recent report of global overeating/heart disease
Made for a very disturbing dental waiting-room read
But as my slave hygienist polished my fangs, I had a comment
Personally (and old Drac agrees), *keep up the greed...*

OOZEMEFLING

Unexpected friendships in your muscle-ache sixties
Is not what you expert in later life
Neighbours helping out become as close as family
As much a pal as your kids or wife

Thingumabob, whatchamacallit and a doohickey
Describe an object or a gadget thing
Our endlessly inventive craftsman neighbour, Lew
Uses made-up words like *oozemefling*

Seven weeks on an outdoor patio has us rebuilding
A formerly fucked-over garden space
Hardcore whackers, cement mixers and powerdrills
Pouring levelling-compound into place

Mounds of clay, chunks of ballast and London Stock
Sit alongside levels, buckets and trowels
Evolving changes to the layout and design mistakes
Often elicited several decorative vowels

Not everything is straight lines and perfect symmetry
On the huff can drive you round the bend
But I will remember with affection the dusty madness
Of mixing *Setcrete* with our creative friend

Life is a funny peculiar whatsit of random transactions
And rising to challenges can be a test
But I thank the good Lord for a world that still surprises
Where collaboration is a welcome guest...

For our neighbour and friend LEW

LOWS & SAVAGE, BIRMINGHAM
(Under Paint Swept)

In a late-onset fit of deep dive home-renovation hysteria
(An anathema to a self-professed DIY reprobate)
I've developed an alarming taste for a quick restoration
Has me sanding and preserving, all things ornate

I took a cranked push barrel bolt off the 1875 front door
And burnt off congealed paint, none too discreet
Only to see an oval plate, *Lows & Savage, Birmingham*
Which when wire-brushed came up a brassy treat

Our neighbours Bob and Angela are helping Mary Ann
Hang wallpaper on the loft landing, exacting lines
The two girls are like Mick and Keith in creative tandem
Complimenting each other's input, better designs

There's a collaboration of smarts and homemaker grit
As they solve the Sanderson's lotus blossom edge
Two women of a certain age with a river of knowhow
Applying elbow grease to the patterned wedge

I'm downstairs by the kitchen sink scrubbing off gunge
Nostalgia for these fantastic brownstones flowing
Were there maids setting the fireplaces every morning?
Brushing surfaces, persevering, hope not showing

Then I think of one hundred years of disparate travellers
Who've passed through this regal pylon of brick?
What was their lot in life? Did they find happiness here?
Maybe their kids rose above the low scullery wick

Is this where we're all headed; lives under-paint swept
Hidden by a poor tradesman at bodge-it-and-go
You make your mark with whatever tin you've at hand
Paint your masterpiece now, *proudly up on show...*

For ANGELA, MARY ANN and BOB
Doing the landing area kitchen unit outside Dean's room
Creative and Practical while I did the front door bolts

MAKE DO AND MEND

It's a glorious sunny Monday (aren't they all), the 20th of April 2020...
But like everyone else on the planet we're locked down tight
With a disease that's killing a surreal thousand a day on TV
Nurse fatalities, even here by the coast in the warm fresh air breeze

My boiler-suited better-half Mary Ann is 62 years of age today
Birthday girl mixing paint in the hallway of our 19th century home
Tail-ending two years of money-pit referberations in Margate

She meant to order Battleship Grey from a German Company
On Jeff Bezos' Amazon.co.uk, doing her bit to make him $10,000
Every Nano second of every minute of every day
Until his online behemoth is now third only to Apple at 1.2 trillion
And snapping at the heals of Microsoft at 1.1 trillion
As the richest business on Earth - a 22% increase in online Sales
Since self-isolation and social distancing killed every high street

But she ordered White in error...
And is now stirring Black paint into the stinky masonry goo
Before going at a first coat on our chipped and worn steps
Leading up to the newly tiled porch of No. 4 Clarendon Road

Like the practical and imaginative trooper she is
A mistake has become an artistic triumph
Mimicking her World War II Dad and Mum (Bill and Rosa) before her
Make do and mend

I'm lying down in the loft room with underlying heart conditions
Avoiding being an unseemly weekend leftover corpse
Trying not to wheeze-and-die from Coronavirus by the fine china

Like everyone else, I'm dazed, in a halfway house dreamworld
Thinking about our three grown-up kids and their future
Worrying about their generation and what we'll bequeath them
As my wife lines up a second coat
To keep that bastard rain from seeping through the cracks
Into Bob and Angela's basement flat below

Turning mistakes into triumphs, adversity into solution
Applying liquid love to yesterday's death-is-all horror story
Taking a tip from those who've been there before and survived
Make do and mend...

RIDING THE BLUE WAVE

We're in the *Blue Wave Hydrotherapy Pool* on a Saturday
The 3:30 afternoon slot for Special Needs is packed
Dean is handling the awkward-moving babies/kid noises
Better now than ever, steady, if overload attacked

The able-bodied teens have no care for rules/boundaries
As they splash and bomb, even when it's forbidden
They glance nervously at twisted limbs and canvas hoists
Like they're radioactivity, diseases formerly hidden

In July 2021, Nutley held a 30th Birthday Party for our Dino
Set out tables with cakes, balloons and cordial jugs
But when one of the bored visitor kids burst an inflatable
A resident freaked out, only sedated by carer hugs

On the Easter Break April 2022, we're sat with Fish n' Chips
Your Meal, Your Way is stencilled on the outer box
The Margate sea air and steel chairs, cold and windswept
Dino eats methodical, tissue-wiping ketchup spots

He's a man now with a long and gangly stretch of bones
As we swish about the coloured water by the jets
Dean lies back confident as I hold up his torso, semi-floats
Even the water gurgling his ears, no longer upsets

On our daily walks by the beachfront at Westgate-on-Sea
He walks ahead of us, loving the wind-in-your face
Dino hand flaps and shouts because there's no one there
A strange kind of peace in its chaos, healer place

A middle-aged man in a wheelchair is pushed by parents
Both old and worn out by a lifetime of pitying stares
Head-braced and gnarled, he grunts uncontrollably loud
But still they smile at him/us in dual empathy shares

So as I hold up a man who will never have kids of his own
And push him around, as the soothing hydro's play
I watch our Dino beam and embrace his organized wave
Pushing out all that noise, floating all the blue away...

For our DINO on his 31st Birthday, 15 July 2022 (resident at Nutley)

BARBARELLA'S CHEW TOY

Life in your Sixties is about moving from svelte lovers
Who once craved every sweaty dalliance in a public lift
To becoming lardy couch friends who need each other

Pals watching other nubiles dry-hump on tables in Netflix shows
Armed with a nice cup of Yorkshire Tea (keep the bag in, if you don't
Mind love) and tremendously well-made sensible Slippers from Lidl

Life in your sixties is about dreaming of Jane Fonda as a 1968 sexpot
Bit by bit undressed by Commandant Durand-Durand (Milo O'Shea)
As she lies dying of orgasmic pleasure in the Excessive Machine
To the backdrop of a manically groovy Psych Soundtrack
That's really saying something man (boy, did she blow his fuses)

It's a bit like that too
At the cake fancies section in Waitrose
When you spot a Strawberry and Cream Éclair
With your calorie-inducing name on it

Serpentine
It sits in a perfectly controlled fridge unit
Coiled, grinning - a slut on a roll
Seducing your slippery Catholicism with superb package presentation

It's the Barbarella Chew Toy
You settle for in your sixties

And glad you still have some original teeth left
After all those boiled sweets in school and cinema flea pits

And with its crisp chocolate topping / dairy-fresh gloop
Aimed at your cavernous open gob

You feel lucky too, tentatively hopeful even
That at our age, and with our past recipes for life
You can chew at all...

CLUSTERED REGULARLY INTERSPACED
SHORT PALINDROMIC REPEATS
(Formerly Known As You And I)

CRISPR is the acronym given to the scientific process of gene splicing
Clustered Regularly Interspaced Short Palindromic Repeats in full
You can now have variants of me even better than the fabulous last
Minus verbal diahorrea, B.O./flatulence, no quoting Catholic bull

Should you require irksome creativity or popular deficiencies erased?
Google FRANK E. STEIN & Associates, please don't hesitate to ask
For we will guarantee you a more alarmingly calm Mark Gerard Barry
There is no personality trait or physical irritants too difficult to task

Should you need to tether unruly offspring, even cancel imaginations
Please fill in our online cash-generating personal info-sharing app
We will simply splice out their former disturbing individualism and traits
And replace them with soft new woke variants, a compliant sap

So as we move forward into a brave new age of edited superhumans
Please excuse me if I prefer go old school, age naturally and die
And when we look back at our egomaniacal scientific advancement
Maybe shed a tear for individuals, formerly known as *'You and I'*...

EINSTEIN AFTER THE EVENT

We pay a truly terrible price for fear in life

Decades of half-existence; where, like some badge of honour
We stoically carry around all that crap nurturing the crippled-inside
The shit we just don't deal with
Sap City in Sucker House - ring the second-chance bell on the left
But do it meekly darling, don't want to upset the ravenous rats
Nor the powder puff neg woodworm resting during daylight hours

Each gender has the same sob story

The girl you didn't ask to dance
The boy you pined after but couldn't approach
The job you never applied for; the book you couldn't publish
The creativity you feared to show the world
The bullyboy in the schoolyard, in the workplace, in relationships
The screenplay you didn't post despite promises you made to children

Is my globule paunch woke enough to show its truth in polite society?
Should I venture an opinion that hasn't been vetted by Talk Radio?

The junk jukebox of life plays debilitating grooves on auto-repeat
Who is that shape-shuffling fucker who thinks he's in his 40s or 50s
With his leaning Tower of Pisa gait that I don't recognise anymore
And who notices his chest-dent now, his previous cut eyebrows
The emotional thick lips and bloodied noses of the past

The cool sea breeze of hindsight wafts across knuckleheaded decisions
Where past mistakes are not carried over in the long division of survival

So just as I'm looking in the mirror post another predictable stumble
I'm asked by a friend for advice; wisdom of years; instruction poultice

So I say, honestly man - *confront the cunt* – shut up with the excuses
Step up to the demarcation line and step down off that train of pain
Throttle all of those finagling Nazis in their Bundersgarden briar-sty
Ring Bell No.1 in *Freedom Lodge*...and not No.2 in *Sucker House*

Be Awkward, Be Untoward, Be a Colditz Tunnel
But don't ever be *Einstein After The Event*...

SIGNIFICANT OTHERS

Every parent wants the best for their children
But few of us ever witnesses the moment their destiny arrives...

June 2009, Year 6, Aged 11
St. Mary's Catholic Junior School, Shernhall Street, London E17
Our son Sean George is starring in his first Stage Play *Bugsy Malone*
And Master Simmons-Barry has landed the plum Lead Role
Playing the all-singing all-slugging Mini-Me Mobster

We sat nervous at first - then we sat stunned
Arms in the air, our shy-lad - gone
Enunciating to the audience as if he owned the Hall
Suddenly fearless, commanding, charismatic
Exuding extraordinary confidence
And as he stood there, centre-stage, I could see it in Sean's face
The emergence of himself through the life force of others
Stepping out of the shadow-past onto a new path ahead

After the show I met his animated teacher in the hallway
I looked at Mister Doherty in as much shock as he gawked back
"Where did that come from? Did you see *that*?"
Unspeakably proud, I blurt, "Beats the shit out of me! And I'm his Dad!"

Doherty laughed out loud at my crude honest response
But I could see that he too was lit up like a Christmas tree
Tingling with a good teacher's natural intuition
Something magical had just happened
Something special – a lightning-rod moment emerging...

...Out of the pulverized corner of existence's boxing ring
Had come a natural ability to tell tales, summon up histories
A conduit to fears and hopes and dreams and longings
Finding voices and illuminating stories
A character gunslinger, holstering the emotional Slug Fest that is Life

And now 24 years of age, but better equipped (better duds too)
Our bold lad stands on another stage, inhabiting new *Significant Others*
Channelling smoke-wisps of the human experience
And with a fair shake at greatness, shimmering in the sexy distance...

For our son, SEAN FRANCIS

TIDDLEY OM POM-POM

A working class holiday in a seaside town used to be the rage
Hop on the train, jump in the car; lung health restore
Banging out Music Hall Shanties about strolling along the prom
On the Dodgems, Chair-O-Plane, Waltzers and more

You get a penny-push cacophony in the Amusement Arcades
As all the machines and teddy-grabs vie for attention
Screamers pack the Helter Skelter, Roller Coaster, Ferris Wheels
Kids on painted Gallopers whoop at parental mention

But, *do I like to be beside the seaside* with its urinal seaweeds
And Kamikhazi seagulls hand-nicking my greasy chips
All manner of flesh grots in disturbingly tight budgie smugglers
None exactly critiquing on Shakespearian Sonnet clips

We've watched Margate rise from the ashes of notorious hole
To the must-see must-visit destination of youthful choice
Tracey Emin started the ball rolling, but it's Down From London
Types and their flush equity has given this mute a voice

The old town housed staggering drunks and hopeless addicts
Darting from punter to punter bumming each for coin
But gradually as the closed shops took on new young owners
Tables and chairs appeared, customers began to join

Soul Boys and the PRIDE community too have taken it to heart
Everywhere bustles with their colour, invention and fun
Soon scaffolding wrapped around every towering Town House
Turned into feature-depleted HMO flats, regen begun

Five years ago this town was a dead zone and going nowhere
And gentrification took its time; now I honestly confess
Yes *I do like to be beside the seaside* with every type of person
Splashing about in all this crazy-beautiful cultural mess...

For MARGATE TOWN and all its Tiddley Om Pom-Poms

HIDING IN PLAIN SIGHT
(Sweets and Streets)

Convalescing with a Marguerita and Strawberry Cream Cake
I was unceremoniously accosted by a Surgeon/NHS bill
I glanced down at the cost of my 75-day stay in two hospitals
It didn't give my accountant an erectile monetary thrill

So now its all salads and exercise and watching what I gobble
No more naughty snacks or Season bingeing Jaffa Cakes
No chomping down on a jumbo bag of Sea Salt and Vinegar
Inbetween Dark Chocolate Bars and other 85% mistakes

A self-inflicted stupidity is hilarious in the afterglow of hindsight
Although your children and terrified wife may disagree
Laughing at cheesecakes and Coconut-Covered Ice Cream
And how I almost didn't make to the ripe old age of 53

But sometimes I flashback to my quad bi-pass torturing ordeal
Hurt-shit you'd supressed by way of mental self-defence
I think about the early morning of the operation in the shower
An orderly shaving both legs; humiliated, ragged, tense

Then I think about cutesy animated Polar Bears targeting kids
White Mama cuddling her cub with a Red Bottle of Coke
And a Black pastor on US TV riling against obesity/T2 diabetes
Sweets killing more parishioners than bullets, a sicko joke

So now I review every label for unsaturated fat percentages
The small print literally obscuring eye-watering amounts
Evil hiding in plain sight; I walk past reams of sly valve closers
And remember that blade, sap-avoiding when it counts...

THE SLOW UNDOING
(Judas Prevailed)

Is this how evil wins? How our fundamental rights get eroded?
Religious zealots institutionalising sicko Gilead hate?
In the USA on 24 June 2022, SCOTUS overturned a 1973 ruling
Giving all women a safe way to early on terminate

Now even in the case of rape or incest, the insemination stays
Regardless of the outcome or the grotesque at fault
This sickening rollback of a person's rights is all Republican led
Trump and his Supreme Court's sly backdoor assault

They've thrown women at the mercy of gutless male politicians
Kowtowing to hard right groups who despise all gays
They aim to legally control what you cherish or even believe in
As long as it fits into indoctrination that blindly obeys

I cannot believe that a panel of nine unelected superior types
Has culled the rights of a woman to personal choice
Fifty years of the landmark advancement that's Roe vs. Wade
Thrown in humanity's dustbin by a God-centric voice

In January 1961, newly elected JFK gave his Inaugural Speech
When he said, "We are the heirs to that first revolution...
Unwilling to witness or permit *the slow undoing of human rights*
Bear all for the success of Liberty" his eloquent solution

Well now, in the United States of Chaos, in a Far Right America
There's been a different coup; progress finally curtailed
A woman's right to choose shot down by five unelected rapists
What was once haven is now home to Judas prevailed...

THE THINGS WE'VE HANDED DOWN

Local kids and their animated parents come rambunctious calling
Giggling tee-hee in Halloween refinery and treat gathering bowls
Sporting plastic-print skeleton aprons and Frankenstein neck-bolts
Dracula capes and demented pointy Stevie Nicks witch hats

Traversing the ten steps up to our lit pumpkins brownstone doorway
When you open up wide with bucket in hand, they shout *Trick or Treat!*

Sprats only ever want the sweets they recognise (no Satsumas mister)
Wrapped chocolate whirls, raspberry ripples, whole nuts, toffee bricks

The pushier-ones Dyson-hoover your outstretched tin of Quality Street
While the meek ones trundle up from behind, accepting sloppy seconds
But I watch out and allocate them some extras (to the smiles of carers)
All enjoying a community tradition that stretches back decades
The things we've handed down...

No worries here of a cannula stuck in our son's vein in a hospital A&E
Because his Autism is now producing late onset full Epileptic seizures
No Stage 4 diagnosis here for my sister in Dublin whose cancer is back
Chemo, time frames, aggressive pain management, texts to relatives
Friends who've also endured losses and heartbreaks and still stood tall

I think of my Father John taking a Recovery Call from a nervous sufferer
My strong and savvy Mum Maureen tackling the mad nuns for Frances
Cathy, Damien and Jonathan laughing at the kitchen table about films

Heartbreak as our young mongrel Skipper got knocked down by a car
Sweaty as we walked back from the Grove Dance on a summer night
The music that had lifted up our lives, slow clinches to 10cc and Joni M
Maybe our kids will one day get to taste the same magic, only different
Good times and bad - things handed down...

One child who has clearly made a huge effort with her outfit is sobbing
Last two times around, she got shoved and didn't get any candy treats
Her mother hunkers down to level four and brushes back her curly hair
"Don't worry sweetheart – you'll get another chance – yes you will!"

Her daughter seems unconvinced at first, but at our neighbour's door
Mum steps up and whomps two barging boys and their grabby hands
Minnie Minx immediately regains her spunk and forgets her former pain
Dancing with her crew now to the next gift-giving cobweb door

And I see Mum look at her girly with such unspeakable pride and joy
Her every gesture filled with the ancient flow of family and parenting
Love invested – love realised – recovered and strong - love living on
In the things we've handed down...

For our friends NIAMH, SAOIRSE and OONAGH DEVLIN

SQUEAKING BUNKBEDS
(Danno Will Be Pleased)

I'm like every other Joe Public when it comes to the law
I want villains shanked and their assets squeezed
Detective Steve McGarrett (Jack Lord) in Hawaii Five-O
Shouting Book 'em! Thus keeping Danno pleased

I'm about the Playtex Girdle approach to cold criminals
Strangle their private parts with maximum control
I want my bad guys to be thrown in solitary confinement
Where the bunkbed squeaks by a poo-poo bowl

Sporting a machine gun twice the size of Massachusetts
Sly Stallone dispenses his Rambo justice and guts
With bulging biceps and a fetching red jungle bandana
Saving the exploited in Deer Hunter bamboo huts

Arnie sorted out The Predator, Ripley bitch-slapped Alien
While Luke Skywalker was forceful with his Dad
Columbo washed his overcoat, then phoned her indoors
As Sherlock Holmes fiddled on Moriarty's bad

But let's go back to the hornary old days of The Sweeney
When system wrong-uns were a doddle to spot
Throw them in some dungeon with fifteen BBC controllers
And let the whole rat-fuck paedo cesspool rot

But it's more likely we get more penalty charge dispensers
Working parking softs for council dosh on the sly
Than any urban hero standing on a perch in a black cape
Swooping down on the city filth from a Bat-lit sky

We're a long way from opportunistic maniacal stereotypes
When Cop TV Shows oversimplified our daily fight
But we take our comfort in knowing that out there still lurks
One Danno (James MacArthur) doing what's right...

BANGING THE POTS
(Beautiful Rosie)

On Duncan Raban's *Just Say Hello* YouTube steam of videos
Is an interview he held with a London WWII survivor
Beautiful Rosie (as she was known) had left school aged ten
Foraged for wood down by the river, imp conniver

Duncan is a bit of a likely-lad himself and conducive chitchat
Loves to find characters on the streets, hear stories
The former photographer of Rock 'n' Rollers/Music Celebrities
Left glam behind in 2004 to capture *people* glories

In his travels, Duncan met the 91-year-old irrepressible widow
Regaling her ballsy youth, never was shy with blokes
She was in bars aged 15, then dancehalls jitterbugging tunes
Make up and clothes made her older, lipstick coax

Aged 18, the Italian-looking dark-haired babe was a magnet
And soon nabbed a hubby, blushed at equal hots
He knew he was in for some action when kitchenware rattled
Banging on cooking utensils, especially boiling pots

She survived cancer three times, but could do no more chemo
Still cheered up when asked, what is the secret of life
She said *"Make love every day…"* laughing heartily at camera
And *"kindness"* is the healer during isolation and strife

Her stories of survival, homelessness, the Circle Line to stay warm
Reflected a generation that faced down every jive
And as she sat there thinking of her former glory days of sharing
You could see that libido wasn't sin; it kept love alive

So God Bless You *Beautiful Rosie* taken by Covid-19 in Feb 2021
I'll bet you're up there, knocking spots off every guy
Rocking a mini-skirt, coyly acknowledging the wild wolf whistles
As you tear it up, on that great dancefloor in the sky…

For BEAUTIFUL ROSIE who passed 13 February 2021
And Duncan Raban's YouTube Video Interviews

STOGIES and STILETTOS
(Average Joe and the Absolute Bomb)

Our hankering for the certainties of yesteryear is now obsession
An entire industry cranking out perfect, the good old days
But if we're not careful to acknowledge that oddity is also love
We will miss the messy things that set our trajectory ablaze

I'm reminded of Humphrey Bogart when he met his lady Lauren
He was 43 years of age and she was an ingénue of only 19
They met on the Howard Hawks movie - *To Have And Have Not*
And developed a nervous rapport, giggling scene-to-scene

Bogey was on marriage number three and his jealous wife knew
Stabbed him in an alcoholic rage, studio hushed up the dirt
But when filming ended in May 1944, Bogey wrote to his passion
"I die a little in my heart when I walk away..." - genuine hurt

Slim and Steve (their nicknames from the movie) married in 1945
Twenty-five years her senior, barely any of hers approved
They had two children together, but cancer took him early at 56
She was a widow at 32, her legendary devotion unmoved

Things were simpler in the past; even Average Joe found his love
Didn't matter if his face was a bag of hammers, mutated
It was all nodding Trilbys and swishing frocks, Stogies and Stilettos
Creased pants in flannel suits, sexy high-heels, celebrated

Perhaps we long for movie romance, precisely because it's corn
All mouth and mumbles and crumpled like our Humphrey B
But I hope our siblings shiver with chemistry, when their lover says
Ill-fitted palooka or no, you're the *absolute bombshell to* me...

For all the Great Romances/Romancers, on-screen and off

COLD WATER APPRENTICESHIP

I've been basking in long hot showers for most of my life
Warming up my weary road-frozen bicycle bones
But now in this final carcass of compromised circulation
I'm turning that hot dial toward unthinkable zones

Bravura feeds the old grey matter of us Sixties pensioners
Still countenancing our wild thirty-something days
But time and reality has bludgeoned paid-in-full stamps
On the passports of former Fatty Arbuckle ways

I'm now jolting the tum flab with aquatic defib paddles
Cascading freeze jets pounding my au natural
I allow my heart beat like a Guantanamo jackhammer
Now that waterboarding torture is my latest pal

I watch two local nutters go swimming in late December
Eagerly discussing next month's east-beast chill
They urge me to take off all my clothes and dive in Mark
Enjoy our outdoorsy Kent Coastal sewage spill

I smile and nod and quickly make my scar-chest excuses
Waving goodbye to exit shrieks and toweling hour
And cheer myself up by looking forward to shrivel prunes
In my very own Scandi Where Eagles Dare shower

So embracing this regimen of cold water apprenticeship
I stand with my arms folded beneath a freezing flue
Never fearing short circuit in my dicky coronary fusebox
When I turn that red tap toward brass monkey blue

We take our health and happiness too much for granted
As if both will be commonly available to us forever
So next time round I'll pray that karma and reincarnation
Improves my mind, my waistline and the weather...

EACH VICTORY IS A WORTHY WIN

Love will conquer all and the universe will provide
What a crock of hippy shit
Spoken by people who've never been paralyzed
In an emotional cess of pit

Mental depression is a clinging pervasive bastard
Weary hard to shake if off
Your dying inside and a voice of wisdom suggests
A dismissive tickly cough

Trust in love to conquer all that's thrown before it
Such a patronising thing to say
Better to arm yourself with a practicality weapon
To drive racing thoughts away

Peer pressure, jobbing stress and relationship abyss
Pour on the demon dark within
Religion and conformist society want pigeonholes
Obsessing over past original sin

I thank Recovery for the tools of the mental trade
Helped me fight my way back
And wish its self-help form of universal practicality
On your next grip panic-attack

Symptoms may be uncomfortable but not dangerous
Was the mantra I hammered in
I may be plagued with nervous crap that fucks me up
But each victory is a worthy win...

For *RECOVERY, INC.*
Formed by Dr. Abraham Lowe to provide practical help
To those with debilitating nervous conditions

KEEP IT RIGHT THERE Y'ALL (Average White Boys)

When I reminisce on sweaty nightclubs and megawatt speakers
Keeping it right there y'all as we hit the floor to dance
I recall some seriously tortured moves masquerading as stepping
Heaps of us white R&B lovers shaking ants in our pants

We'd boogie all night to Earth, Wind And Fire, Chaka and Prince
Twelve-Inch singles extending the Nile Rodgers groove
Flaying beats until we dropped, our hips contorted, dogs barking
Trying to woo a girl with your Average White Boy move

But there's nothing dismissible about the Soul and Funk we loved
The 70ts & 80ts sound, still the staple of many FM stations
Will we ever see another Motown, Stax, Atlantic; Warner Brothers
All those fabulous songs, messages, uptempo creations

Maybe we are old and in the way, should bugger off, move it on
Stick old Aretha Franklin, Bill Withers and Stevie Wonder
But I'm never going to stop listening to their fantastic Soul legacy
Marvin's sexy genius, stirring up the rhythm down under...

For SOUL BOYS and GIRLS and DANCERS everywhere

THE FUTURE IN HIS FACE

In the left luggage of precious memories, I cherish the one
Where Julia and I watched Austen with Walkers Crisps
Sat on the couch bingeing on all six episodes of the BBC's
Pride & Prejudice, Darcy exiting a lake with soggy nips

Steven Spielberg's Jurassic Park blew her teenager noggin
With its effects and scare-you-shitless T.Rex mucky foot
She has a tattoo now on her arm of that rampaging brute
Others too in unmentionable areas, tastefully inky soot

But of all the Rom Coms and Action Adventures watched
None so obsessed as when The Notebook went on air
Ryan Gosling and Rachel McAdams as Noah and his Allie
James Garner and Gena Rowlands as the elderly pair

They argue and laugh and kiss passionately in downpours
Engaging in all sorts of gymnastically romantic mush
Until later she's got Alzheimer's and slow loss of memories
So he reads from their diary, the healing echoes rush

I saw then what so many fans like our JuJu have longed for
The young and old versions of a keeper, still in place
As Noah braves the bar of a Ferris wheel, dangling fearless
Smiling at the prize that is Allie; *the future* in his face...

For our daughter JULA HOPE

LEANING INTO CORNERS

Heading home on this air-conditioned bullet
To sadness and undertow

I like train journeys, blur-and-stir scenery
Kissing-windows that glint (softly on the cheek kisses)
Majestic infusions of nature, each suddenly washing over you
Like hot buttered toast and window-seat tea sups
And the foliage too, and the trees, and the inviting pastures, all of it

It's like we haven't noticed it in our diminishing middle-aged dotage
And then suddenly we're hit with earthy reminders of what's important
And not what's driving emotional nails
Into our over stimulated media skull-screwed headspaces

Even now, in late November, when it's undeniably bleak and cold
With miserable greyness that reminds you of bullies in schoolyards
There's still something old-world magical about it
Nature nurturing, landscapes that have always provided and lasted
Framed by the pipe and slippers swish of this lean into corners tube
Buffeting the sometimes cruel turns in life, out there, in the real world...

Our beloved father John Francis Barry is lying prostrate in hospital
A stroke having paralysed the right side of his 86-year old face
An inoperable tumour in the oesophagus pressing on his larynx
Making eating painful and narrowing survival to weeks, not years

I join the ventilators, drips and cardiac monitors whirring and bipping
In that clinically detached way, applied but removed (like us)
In a foggy netherworld of parental passing and sibling wreckage

Doted on by angel nurses in Dublin's Beaumont Hospital
And tended to by family and his wife Maureen of nearly six decades
A final stretch after 8-years of Bone Marrow Cancer injections to
Now, puking up 36-tablets onto the lino, his body saying, *enough*...

Once out of industrialised Euston and on our way to Holyhead
09:15 soon reflects a more gentile order, memories of jam and clay
Tilled soil, pert muck lines from tractor tracks, livestock grazing fields
Leeway rills, windswept tufts of nettle and briar, bales of recently mown
Hay rolled up like giant Shredded Wheat Swiss Rolls, and all of it
Ominously overseen by strangely still crows on bare branches

Line after line, scoping the idyll, like a firing squad with no feelings...
Suits with laptops alight at Milton Keynes, always leaving discards
Chatty housewives tut at 1st Class ticket holders getting on at Chester
None-to-subtle power dressers shaping past every numbered seat
Like they're Royalty and you're gulping their valuable oxygen intake

Provincial train stations pass with long unpronounceable names
Workingmen in highly visible ill-fitted yellow jackets clip grass ridges
Allotment squares hog bamboo dividers and dirty mini glasshouses
Seagulls alight on worm-clay behind a lone no threat slow plough
Gangly protruding pylons walk like girder giants, mad and marauding

And then there's the oddbods, the driven types, nervous but nice
Men with timetables and binoculars that jump on board at Crewe
Watch canal barges navigate the extraordinarily narrow waterways

They monitor increasing speed, turn their apertures, focus quick
Catch one last sight of something beautiful that's survivor ancient
An arched stone footbridge, straight out of Tolkien's Middle Earth
A simple transitional thing that helps get us from one place to another

I'm the first born, September 1958, a Sunday's child
My lovely wife Mary Ann has herself battled Stage 3 Breast Cancer
Me, still reeling from a Quadruple Heart Bi-Pass when I turned 54
Both of us feeling like we dodged some kind of karma shotgun shell
But here I am, watching charming British countryside go by
Staving off chasms and yet oddly relieved

I've been dreading this moment, this journey, prayer-hoping for
No more needles, nor transfusions, nor cannulas, no more pain...

Dad would have loved this gorgeous landscape view
In his quiet taking-it-all-in kind of way
The serene abutting the ugly, mirroring the mess of life
Probably won't like the cards son, but play the hand you're given
As he might once have joked, him and Mum always equipping us

I love train journeys
And I have my Stax Records paperback too *Respect Yourself*
(A mantra he would have approved of)
Although I know I won't be able to bring myself to actually read it
Not on this final passing, not now...

As we near Holyhead and Welsh countryside melts into wisp salt
I think about the last time I saw my Dad up and about, able
Standing alone in the Irish Ferries car-park as Ulysses docked
Me up on the rear outer decks, waving, knowing his shape

So glad he was there, my lovely father, welcoming me home
And here I am again at Ferry Port, Dublin
But his familiar gait isn't there to greet me
The rest of the family at the hospital, trying to help

Me then turning to make my way down to the disembarkation area
Where, once inside, stood by the heavy weather-shielding doors
And despite the warmth and safety of the inner decks
And as I went down the stairs to my ancestral home

A sudden crow shiver came over me

And then again, another
As I sat their in those limbo seats in the exit-deck area, waiting

And I knew what it was. I know six years down the line, what it is.

I must be real, endure, accept what is to come and lean into
Fresh air and the open sea and the life-giving sunshine outside

Our loved ones waving at us
Wishing us footbridges and good luck and safe passage

As they move on without us
Fade into memory shadow
Embracing the spectacular view from a different platform
We're not yet allowed to step upon...

For JOHN FRANCIS BARRY
My Dad, who passed 7 December 2015 in Dublin, Ireland
With love and huge respect from all his extended family and friends

KISSING SCARS IN THE SECOND HALF

Full-on cancer treatment is physically brutal and cruel
Her confidence shot and whole body battered
She's sliced and vulnerable and feels like a meat tray
Her head-turning babe days surgically tattered

We inhabit an image-conscious youth-obsessed world
Where the young never think of the second half
As we get older and the lack of earlier smarts manifest
Bellies and diseases replace the shrug off laugh

There are reasons why marriage vows elicit a response
Of running in the self-centred generational new
You commit to someone for all their physical chapters
Though health and monitors and the razor crew

Obsessing on who wants whom and who now doesn't
Is not an exit strategy in the lifetime marital deal
Love is having each other's back, caressing damages
Kissing scars where there was once flesh to feel...

For our MARY ANN and all those fighting THE BIG C

WAITING FOR THE KINGFISHER

We're in *Stodmarch National Nature Reserve* five miles past Canterbury
A really pretty part of Kent steeped in marshes and binocular hides
Where the late summer sun is still catching the constantly pitted water
The River Stour's flow like a nightclub glitterball zapping all that moves
Eliciting the infectious giggling of teenagers skyscraper-high on life

I'm stood motionless because I'm waiting, hoping for another glimpse
Of the Kingfisher whose built a hole-nest in the slightly raised mud bank
Just to our left, a short ways away from a dive branch above the team

She's already departed it once for a beak-full of minnow
A silver streak gusto whacked and stripped with precision
Din-dins for her chicks undoubtedly sheltering within
The most incredible bright-blue layer coat, copper-orange underbelly
And a fidget dance that invites delight, even whooping awe

Although the moment I saw this luminous creature was fleeting
Its deeper impact crept up on me afterwards
The violin note serenity of its hummingbird flit across the spiked reeds
The polished finesse in its dive, retrieval and care of its young

Ancient sailors used to say Kingfishers even calmed the raging tempest
Quelled the unnerving winds, placated monsters lurking up ahead
Shadows that threatened to swallow all of them whole

And I'm reminded; I see the face of a nine-year old grinning at camera
Tomato sandwiches in her school lunchbox, hummus too
Standing proudly by her proper wooden violin in its protective case
Billie 'Holiday' Clayton, twin to Edward, daughter to Yorkshireman Ian
And her Punk Rock sweetheart mum Heather

I see her gorgeous happy face - by this river - skimming stones at first
But then, by the calm of summer water
Resin polishing her stringed pride and joy
Getting its limitless music ready for visitors who will be coming soon

Who will so glad to see her, reduced to tears and trembling
At the sight of something so utterly beautiful...

For BILLIE 'Holiday' CLAYTON and her Kingfisher Family

NOT EXACTLY BRANDO, GETTING CLOSE TO BACALL

Clearly punching above his goofy weight with Ms Maureen Wolfe
Dad eyed his intended at a Balgriffin corrugated dance
Introduced and chaperoned by her best friend Ms Maura Molloy
Our parents began an unlikely, but well-suited romance

In his handmade suit, John F. Barry wasn't exactly Marlon Brando
Posing for wedding photos next to Dublin's Lauren Bacall
Our Glamorpuss Mum embracing that gurgling lifetime cauldron
With a decent man, glad to make that commitment call

Each generation has that photograph they stumble on in boxes
Parents starting out a journey that will flicker hot and cold
Siblings admiring a newly minted couple making plucky choices
Wondering what its like to be so all-in and fire-eating bold

Will our children walk arm-in-arm down a flower-festooned aisle?
In hellacious clobber eliciting congregational drops of jaw
But laughing on the inside, as their besties focus their iPhone 25s
Digitising the newest luddites rocking a fashionista faux pas

As a keen photographer, Dad's glue-paged photo albums grew
Building as door-notches catalogued us moving past play
Prams and schools and jobs, and even more Herculean nuptials
Moments captured for future generations, squirreled away

There's a black and white photo of our Mum on her honeymoon
Walking a Donegal beach looking like a Vogue cover wow
I know what my Dad felt, what his face registered behind the lens
Traded up big-time, awesome woman, got lucky, *and how...*

For my Mum, MAUREEN BARRY-WOLFE (Nanny Mo)
With thanks and respect for a lifetime of love and guidance given

CLIVE JAMES WOULD APPROVE

Aware he was running out of time for righteous poetry
Clive James damned the decorum torpedoes
The revered Australian wit, lyricist, critique and author
Purged his ink of glib, donning truthful Speedos

His earlier verses reflected vast academic knowledge
But you could *feel* his desire to dazzle, impress
2015's *Sentenced To Life* chronicled a gut embracing
Of onset disease, bowl of goof-beautiful mess

In his final years (passed in November 2019), his verse
Ran molten with an honesty and lust for living
Through hospitals and needles and eventual disability
CJ craved relevance, a legacy worth giving

Artistry, design, function, and serious verbal panache
Aren't actually that difficult to wordy institute
But to do so with accessibility, intelligence and heart
Requires real avoidance of conjured-up-cute

Soaking up his unorthodox rhymes every night in bed
And truthfully, some pieces, better than others
Besotted with women, he twigged early their miracle
Bettering him, purge what male ego smothers

James spent a lifetime reading, pampering the mind
Knowledge and learning thrilling his Ozzie DNA
His themes are about love, sex, family and the sprogs
Enthusiastically catalogued their odd interplay

But what moved me most about his last elegiac years
Was an acknowledgement of equal carer pegs
It's the women in your life that are the glue and paste
When our old macho descends into body dregs

Suave Clive would probably chuckle at awed eulogies
And yet be genuinely mortified if he hadn't any
So I imagine him giggling with lady lovers in the afterlife
Saying their investment was worth every penny...

THAT SLY DARKNESS
(Beating Captain Neg)

We're all on a formation journey spanning decades
With our fear dry-humping every emotional leg
But it's survival-important to remember to embrace
A strategy to scupper the slide of Captain Neg

Facing up to the daily blunt trauma of the real world
Is fraught with all manner of invitational triggers
Yet even though it *feels like* your losing crucial battles
There are ways to beat its sly darkness sniggers

Constantly reinforce yourself with the proven mantra
Should racing thoughts begin their crafty fuss
What you feel is uncomfortable, not life-threatening
Panic attacks subside; they're not dangerous

This simplistic code may come across as an exercise
In glib phraseology, smacks of magazine pout
But its life-saving abilities have to be practiced hard
Drummed into thoughts pre-set to auto doubt

It's uncomfortable, but it isn't dangerous is your key
A technique that suppresses the panic attack
You don't rid yourself of its symptoms, but you cope
The next time that mind trickster sashays back

You may convince yourself that today is penultimate
But remember the darkness said that before
And you didn't die; you didn't implode or evaporate
You got through it, not beaten, here, *secure...*

For our daughter JULIA HOPE

DROPSY and TEN-BOB NOTES

Are we old like dropsy, cream-top milk and sew-on patches?
Monkey-puzzle trees in front gardens, globule glooping lava lamps
Spending a penny, scraping your butt with sandpaper Izal loo rolls
Old like the 1-2-3 gear-stick and bobbed mudguards of Choppers
Elephant flare jeans, clingy drainpipes, Florins and Ten-Bob Notes?
Rinso, Brillo Pads, Joyces of Cork Strawberry Bars and Gobstoppers
Old and in the way...out of date...and fast approaching out of time...

Or are we wise and jolly hockey-stick survivors of this Eton Mess of life
Looking back at curled black and whites of *so young* honeymooners
Later pushing a laden rapid-fold buggy-stroller in garish holiday threads
Later still with grinning sprogs on beaches, six sandcastle constructions
And a wild-eyed-need to hold back the tide...

A friend of ours phoned on Wednesday afternoon to keep us informed
Of a lung cancer diagnosis months back; endured first round chemo
Finding the second combo of radiotherapy and meds truly gruelling...
By Saturday Michael had died on his way to the loo, lost to wife Marilyn
Too stunned to process it all as real, rushed to a Jewish funeral
Plain coffin, old world dating, friends silent, numb, weirdly sunny...

There's a Bruce Springsteen song opens his 2020 album "Letter To You"
Called "One Minute You're Here" - the next minute you're gone
Lived through the 60ts and in your Sixties; all is about health and money
And the complete lack of both...

Are we living the next 20 years so our kids will not feel such abandon?
Time closing in; hobbling our legacy; no more chitchats, no leeway...

I heard his voice on the phone as I said *smell the roses Michael*
Like I did after the op - and be glad - I heard his chuckle, his realisation
And I also heard his practical wife in the background
Trying to impose on him the truth of his condition
Which like all men's reaction to disease is to park it and ignore

I heard her inner child, her younger self
Turning her head to that incoming sea
That encroaching expanse
And her wild-eyed need to hold back the tide
As she patted her bestest-ever sandcastle on the head
There, there; not to worry...

A RUN ON FARLEY'S RUSKS
(Soother Suckers)

Back in the day, we'd raid the fridge first, then the cupboards
For anything that resembled sugar, processed or no
A brick of roughly-cut, fowl-tasting cheap cooking chocolate
Or some rock hard jelly-square; we were good to go

But when both sisters Fran and Cathy came home from school
They'd hammer my combo sugar-crave number one
A fat-buttered Farley's Rusk, chased by a bowl of Rice Krispies
Its sucrose-sprinkled milk-soup, a liquid hot-cross bun

Growing pains became waistline gains and gym memberships
Battle of the Bulge every time you opened your mouth
Work-snacks and lunchtime-treats and comfort-eating Kit Kats
Saw figure-hugging jeans and shirt tucking gone south

In later years as we visited dentists and the bedrooms of lovers
We gained children, but kissed our pearlies goodnight
So keep your mitts off calorie-killers and your knickers knotted
And remember, only *soother–suckers* eat all that shite...

For my sisters FRANCES and CATHERINE

EXTREME RED HEAT WARNING

An *Extreme Red Heat Warning* has been issued in the UK
For Monday and Tuesday the 18th and 19th of July
The Met Office has warned us of historical temperatures
As many as 10,000 deaths; so damn hot, you'll die

It's the first time 40+ degrees has been forecast in Blighty
As well as *Adverse Health Conditions* up to Level 4
A fire-starter and suffocation killer of vulnerable life forms
Every environmental warning made real and more

Some folks see the grey squirrels skitting across the trees
As flying rodents rather than picturesque to cherish
Others slate the squawking seagulls and nesting chicks
As an environmental cast of turds, meant to perish

Three days ago a fox was found dead on the dirt ridge
Opposite our Margate pad where we park the car
We called the council to remove the decaying carcass
But of course, being actual work, was a job too far

So Angela bagged the body up and Bob disposed of it
Thrown into a Communal dumpster, whisked away
I'll miss him playing of an evening amidst the shrubbery
Mother Nature crying quietly, a species falling prey

Why does red-heat feel like the beginning of our end?
When we've known for so long, world on its knees?
I'll take that dead fox as a sign, zero emissions replace
The scent of evil's triumph, lingering on the breeze...

134

NOISES IN OTHER ROOMS
(The Sound of Broken)

Weary, I'm lying on a double in an unlit bedroom just after Boxing Day

It gets dark as early as four now in these bleak December afternoons
Mary Ann's display of fairy lights illuminating the bottom half of a huge
Sash bay-window declaring goodwill/glad tidings to the world at large
Or at least the hipster people who walk by on Clarendon Road below

Our late-20s Autistic son is fixating as usual on hours of YouTube video clips
Adverts for the enchanted worlds of Brum, The Riddlers and Rosie & Jim
Early learning material for pre-school children, badly recorded videotapes

Dino makes noises at their sounds, wobbly celluloid shivering, squeaking
But it's long since stopped being cute or fun or spirited or even tolerable
It's like a torture drip you can't escape, lying in the darkness, listening to
The sound of broken, our beautiful son lost in his Auttie world loop

Earlier we sat patiently In the Sainsbury Cafeteria at Westwood Centre
Our specific order for him already 35 minutes late, Dean watches each
Waitress bring a tray to other tables, other diners, his frustration table taps
Starring daggers at the visible kitchen area where old cutlery rattles

A neighbour of ours celebrated her 70th birthday surrounded by family
Young at heart and spring full of life, a cheery soul still looking forward

But I feel like a stranger, eating punch-laced trifle, nursing a half lager
Normally chatty, I even feel like people are placating me, tolerating
Strangers hoping you won't talk too much or say something untoward
Nothing too personal please, Mark, keep it light and then politely go

I lie now on the bed in the darkness and pray yet again to a dim deity
Who seems to be out of town at present on more important business

Maybe you'll help the kids with their job searches/relationship troubles
Keep our Dino safe, when we're no longer here to protect him

Maybe answer prayers like you did in my Whipps Cross Room 18 intern
When that addict down the hallway whimpered and cowered
In his handcuffed withdrawal-madness like Bill Syke's cudgelled cur
Then screaming at the top of his lungs
Shredded throat clemency pleading
Some nights for forty-minutes straight...

Five years hence, I lie on another bed in another emotional quarantine
Arms straight, hands tight in my battered lucky robe's pockets
Like I did in that heart-unit in E17
Trying to negate the shred-nerve torture
Waiting for help and mercy to show up

Keeping still, keeping calm, fighting quietly, the drip-feed of
Noises in other rooms...

For the PARENTS and CARERS of loved ones with Special Needs

TWENTY-FOUR HOUR WINDSOR VIRUS
(Know Your Betters)

British Royalty justifies its ludicrous and moneyed existence
By doing supposedly gracious Humanitarian deeds
But if The British Government was doing its electorate right
All of these wrongs would be fixed; no social needs

Image Beneficial Effect is a hugely effective political play
That the British Press should be daily exposing to us
But instead they engage in insufferable *Yes Mam* routines
Bawling out readers as unpatriotic; curtsy and fuss

So the Public is slyly faced with a lethal double whammy
That compromises and kills, authority sat on fence
British Politicians don't query misdirected taxpayer's cash
Then Tabloids frame the betrayal as benevolence

Misappropriation across decades is a hidden Holocaust
Hospitals, special needs units, hospices never built
How many worthy recipients are there on your Civil List?
Payments made? Are its secretive contents - guilt?

The sly temptation on the part of The British Government
Is to provide Royalty with Humanitarianism to do
But this murders British people by keeping things broken
Without you ever knowing why, how or *for who*?

And dare anybody question the unimpeachable Queen
About how she didn't cotton right from wrong
How she didn't know the obvious physical consequences
That lives are saved; ££s put where ££s belong

Having robbed the sick of their money through 'Yes Men'
They return with camera crew to a hospital bed
Smiling beguiling to show the public how much they care
When they're using pain and loss, securing cred

I'm going to murder people living in England by siphoning
Away cashola to unelected aristocratic lechers
And should I be tempted to call out such useless fripperies
I'll chant the Windsor mantra; *know your betters...*

SEDITIOUS PROPHECY
(The Path Of An Artist)

Safety-first parents worried about jobs and the future
Inflicted us with the curse of questioning ambition
Anything artistic doesn't pay the bills and is unrealistic
Creative pursuance akin to ecclesiastical sedition

The Path Of An Artist is filled with doubt and doubters
Smile-placating responses while they sneer inside
Never tell your plans to anyone who doesn't endorse
They feed on wounded visions, dreams that died

I ridiculous, didn't make it, never amounted to much
Is the doubt-mantra, as your aging will depletes
But every trodden cliché has a basis in historical truth
Swallow jibes and emerge stronger from defeats

You turn up to the page, the spindle and the palette
And you trash that fucker with all your inner might
Because if you don't, they won a war, not the battle
And puerile naysayers proved their prophecy right...

For my Mum, MAUREEN BARRY-WOLFE
My wife, MARY ANN SIMMONS
And my Brothers and Sisters, FRANCES, JONATHAN, CATHERINE & DAMIEN
For our kids DEAN, JULIA HOPE and SEAN FRANCIS
Artists all...

DISAPPOINTINGLY HOLLOW

Honesty is this politician's secret, tough tastemakers heralded
Splattered across gush-columns in every slavering trade
Doesn't suffer fools gladly, won't let the buck stop elsewhere
And that's how his enviable reputation has been made

But I saw Slick Willy wear a yellowish shade of a Brooks Brother
Always shirking the Republican's legislation refusal scam
Never going after core betrayal because it would image hurt
Left the American electorate with a zero progress sham

Could have taken on Ku Klux Klan and institutionalized racism
Instead of crying on TV at the victims of handgun scum
And I still hear Aretha Franklin singing that Sam Cooke anthem
But it was an accumulation of zip; change didn't come

Like so many white men and women who saw the USA anew
We thought at last they had a President worth praising
But hardline Republicans kiboshed every policy for advance
So Barrack travelled abroad; Democrats navel-gazing

A 70-million dollar book deal is secured during a second term
As Presidential Medals of Freedom stave off opposition
Springsteen in Music, De Niro in Film and TV's Ellen DeGeneres
Secured this POTUS no aftermath, soft media inquisition

Broke through the racial ceiling, class act compared to Trump
Brought dignity to the office, raised up America abroad
But all I saw was a manipulator who coasted through 8 years
While media, fearing racial backlash chose to applaud

Barrack *looked good* as The US President, but he did no good
Didn't clip the NRS, homelessness, healthcare inequality
And in the end, who was the hypocrite, the real hope crusher?
Because zero legacy looks disappointingly hollow to me…

BIG STRONG TOYS
(For Big Strong Boys)

Because he did the advert for the *Milky Bar Kid* on Irish tele
Seamus O'Rourke was always flush with the greens
Which meant, whilst we'd piddly Woolworths pistols & caps
He'd a *Johnny Seven O.M.A.* designed by marines

From bi-pod legs, the One-Man-Army threw hand-grenades
And clearly cost his one-upmanship folks a packet
With seven gun slots, twelve rubber bullets and massive box
Next to our sulphur poofs, it made a serious racket

But his comeuppance came from an Orange Dumper Truck
Its mighty metal frame made of sterner *TONKA* stuff
"Big strong toys for big strong boys..." their adverts seduced
And for 1970s indestructibility, I couldn't get enough

Years later, we'd meet in Castilla Park with vinyl under arms
And laugh at what was once so sacrosanct for kids
Agree that most of Action Man's extravaganza weaponry
Probably puckered up both our parents dustbin lids

It was never about whose toys were better value for money
Was always ENORMITY got us ego-mutts deranged
And when we grew up, working in offices and boardrooms
TONKA spirit survived, because nothing's changed...

FOREVER PLANE SPOTTING

Just opposite *The Spitfire & Hurricane Memorial Museum*
Sits the *NAAFI Café* on the Manston Road in Kent
After you've taken in both legendary WW fighter planes
Get a chest-hair brew, couple of quid well spent

Itself abutting undulating grass ridges, higgledy car park
It's known as a *Services for the Services* canteen
Even the tablecloth and fancies hark back to the Forties
The walls proud with period memorabilia re-seen

Remnants of cockpits and fuselages from further conflict
Nimrod, Buccaneer, & Lightning, on plinths erect
The Victor, Buy Bonds, Spam, Ration Books, reminders are
In the ethereal DNA of the site, a ghostly respect

Nestled under an angled 1944 German 'VI Flying Bomb'
Is a bench dedicated to *Peter Austen, 1927-2002*
He worshipped at the altar of flying fortresses & aviation
Forever Plane Spotting plaque from his pals, crew

I didn't know the man but spirit overwhelming, I see him
Binoculars and tea flask, inexplicable sonic bond
As those symbols of freedom roared into the maelstrom
Ascending heroic into a Godlike cockpit beyond...

For PETER AUSTEN and all the AVIATORS

WE GOT YOUR BACK

I often wondered did you swim serenely in someone else
A globule inside another woman's tummy sublime
Later run towards your lover at a clock-dial's rendezvous
And launch into his arms, do the emotional climb

Did your briefly formed Ectopic Soul, relocate corporeal?
Fly away into another nurture vessel to be reborn
The one child we weren't allowed to bring up as a family
A life we never saw unfold, your story fabric torn

My first wife was *Jean*, a Northern Ireland Protestant lady
And we met again today 26-years after the event
We talked quietly about the saw-stab randomness of loss
Regrets of youthful inexperience, histories misspent

But today felt like an ending and even a second chance
Both feelings ping-ponging to & fro as we moved
Walking by the seawall with your long-time second hubby
My Mary Ann absent, closure moment approved

Neither of us focused on our respective partners or jabbed
Only what was lost all those painful decades ago
The private hurt we've both buried down deep about you
The family photographs not there, nothing to show

So you run wild and free our wee Ectopic Soul Boy of Love
We wish you only happiness & adventures galore
And as you navigate the bounty paths of life's possibilities
Remember, *we got your back* and so much more...

For JEAN DOOLE and our Lost One

IN THE WIND

I remember you'd giggle uncontrollably on our weekly video calls
Wanting in on the action with your best buddy and house pal Dean
Stephen too, eldest of the group, chaperoning benevolent his two-posse
The Three Special Needs Musketeers supporting each other
In Sunrise House

Today there were wind chimes in the trees at Nutley (as there always is)
When we came to pick up our 30-year old Dino for his Easter break
But they sounded to me like they were actually singing this time
Making a melody, peace-inducing notes, air-tinkling love
A celebration even

Then, stunned, a carer tells us that after two weeks of protracted illness
Nathan, Dean's resident chum of old, had passed away that morning
Spirits down in Oakley House where they'd moved Nate for hospice
A low blow amidst the new flowers of spring suddenly filling every lea

Eighteen years in this beautiful place, kept safe by dedicated souls
Pals at the ready, daily event-calendars and family visits injecting light
Dean putting on your seatbelt in the back seat of the Community Van
Helping in his own way and calling on Frail Smile, even after the move

Collecting rocks and pebbles was your passion, planting web patterns
Forming *Nathan Patches* that everyone admired and bees alighted on

Now, you're placing angular forms in another sheltered garden
All shapes and sizes welcomed, side by side

And sat on a worn bench in the sun
There is no apparatus to return to, no physical to be endured

There are just songs in the chimes and fragrances in the wind
And memories rustling in great canopied-trees
Mama Nature wrapping its gorgeous healing arms around you

Nathan Small, with his friends, sat there in peace
With all the time in the world to soak in
Every exquisite renewal...

For NATHAN SMALL, Family & all his Carers at Nutley Hall in Uckfield
Passed after years of illness, Monday, 11 April 2022

EMPTY BOTTLE CRATES IN FEAR RATTLING DREAMS

Last night in fitful turning, I dreamt I was emptying old bottle crates
A squat milkman unloading his wares in a grimy WW II white apron

Why the fuck was I suddenly in the English Dairy Industry in 1945?
And how was I able to drive a float, when I can't drive at all?

And I also remember thinking *inside* this surreally casual vapour
That I had now stopped dead-bolt mid-street; I was just stood there
Mojo-less, at the edge of an unfolding lurk-danger, a sap looking in
Like a pedestrian accident waiting to happen

Like some out-of-body scene in a Hollywood surgery film
Where an angel is waiting for you by the non-admittance door
And all the relatives are bawling their eyes out in the hall area
Somehow unable to comprehend the screeching flat-line monitor
As desperate staff apply paddles to a non-responsive fleshy lump

I also remember thinking about the milkman's white bottled payload
Dangling in the middle of a suburban scape of bird chirps/rustle leaves
Is he taking back or delivering anew?
Is he giving that home he's heading towards sustenance?
Or is that visitor and his echo tinkling just taking away spent fuel?

And then I vividly remember suddenly taking a think-tangent...
Why hadn't I gotten up earlier in the morning to stop the birds
Pecking through the silver-top foiled lids
Determined to get to the cream bit at the top?
Why hadn't I intervened? Why the deafening muffle-thud of not doing?
Standing in the middle of the street waiting for the inevitable fender
To smash into my legs and my dangling crate
Now suddenly filled with immaculately cleaned bottles
When I hadn't delivered jack shit yet?

And then thinking, if only I'd acted sooner when I had the chance
Then everything (cream tops and health included) would be intact
And I wouldn't be in this hinterland of regrets and inaction
In this post-mortem quietly-menacing haze-scape

With bottle empties and fear rattling dreams...

INTERRUPTED BY LIFE

Our wings clipped, Festive Season has been cold and short this year...

It's near midnight on Christmas Eve and the fast train from Kings Cross
Is stuck eight stops away - stationary, locked doors, our juvvies inside
Weary, texting, an hour's delay to endure or maybe even more
And all because some little *brätwurst* has clipped cables down the line
So an Engineer (on call) has to be dragged out into the freezing night
While two dedicated workers continue to patrol eerie Margate Station

10:30 p.m., I talk to both Fathers who should be at home in Birchington
And yet stay on to man the wind whipped black-as-loss platforms
So passengers and family can reunite in safety...

Our Julia and Sean are aged 25 and 21 and crap is robbing us of them
New jobs that must be worked, potential customers organically wooed
Eagerness and team spirit noted (are you a hip 5 or an uncommitted 4)
Like some episode of Black Mirrors that smacks of being *all too real*...

Me; do I call it *Boxing Day* like the English do or is it *St. Stephen's Day*
Like the rampant indoctrinated Irish Catholic in me suspects I should?
At 61, I hardly know these days, caught between two land magnets
Old Home there and *New Home* here, alternate realities whispering

We're only getting them for Christmas Day, one lousy day, a glimpse
Then our kids are back to the big choke to meet the Boxing Day Sales
Both young'uns hauled in to candlelight grind the big corporate wheel
That must keep on earning and churning and feeding its greed...

So, 06:30 a.m., on Boxing Day, with a facecloth and streaked chamois
I wipe down the windows of our side-battered Stepway car in darkness
(Better vision for Mary Ann on the four-lane motorway up to London)
And I wave them off, my crew, unable to conceal chest burst pride...

Back inside, on the morning after telly is a redeemed Ebenezer Scrooge
Filled with the milk of Human Kindness and Seasonal Spirit
Standing in the doorway of Bob Cratchit's family home
With a humungous Christmas Dinner Turkey and a smile of gratitude

Love emanating from his every pore, pulled from the darkness
By spectral glimpses, reminders of what he may have lost but still has...

BUZZ ALDRIN

In an unusually non-conformist grey blouson jacket
Afternoon nattering In Burgerland
There's a young woman of 22 with oval glasses
Talking to an older guy of maybe 24

His low-key bomber-top is only slightly zipped up
Faded jeans, brand new velvet boots and thick glasses
The ensemble makes him look intellectual and deep
Not like a flash-stud poser, but subtle, sure
Buzz Aldrin to Neil Armstrong
He's not the first man on this moon, but he is there
Steady and true, got your back

From my point of view, two seats away
The plastic garish yellow table cuts them in half

He's leaning forward a lot now, towards her
Intent and attentive and listening
She's hunched up tight, elbows on what can be a slippery slope
Empty polystyrene burger boxes and French Fries cardholders
Long since cleared away by swoop-and-hoover staff

They're discussing things, talking about life, exploring topics
Endlessly discussing and exploring

She glances every now and then up from the wiped Formica
And stares directly into his eyes, those slim windows
Behind those out-front chunky-rimmed protectors

He responds by leaning forward more, but ever so slightly
Not pushy, not grab, but cautiously
As they discuss things, talk about commonalities and stuff...

On top she's composed, attentive and studious

Underneath, her once tired right foot
Crossed over her stationary left ankle
Is flicking like mad

VICIOUS GENDER
(Arrogance as Cool in the Saving Game)

Testosterone and male machismo 4K-retina our TV screens
With their deriguere *arrogance as cool* not far behind
We seem to have arrived at a place where all Heroes are
Preposterous fantasy-figures, comic clichés redefined

But I don't see men saving this world of ours from extinction
Our political track record is a long brute litany of pain
If men can leverage, fleece or subjugate people/resources
Historically our planet's trashed for exploitation's gain

Child molesters, rapists, drug lords, dictators, flesh traffickers
This is an appalling track record for our vicious gender
If Man is made in God's image as the Holy Scriptures tells us
Then no angels are living here, halo returned to sender

It is women (and always has been) that nurture and protect
Women who make smarter decisions; feel real empathy
The problem is that we're out of time and fast approaching
Being out of luck, precipice, tipping point, the lava sea

They have trusted us for millennia and we've betrayed that
Never offered equality or protected life's continuance
It's time for them to stop trusting us and take over the deck
Dance to humanity; bench our world-killing arrogance

Across a stage of male world leaders, little offers us comfort
Instead it's a shit-show of territorial greed and little men
Who knows if we'll make it past the next environmental cull?
Another gain undercut with the stroke of a fountain pen

But I do know that when the avoidable flood-engulf comes
It won't be a man reassuring, owning rhetorical blame
He'll be on a podium spouting bullshittery while women cry
Could have saved us all had *they* run the saving game...

MOTHER LODE
(Screen Out The Sorrow)

I've a six-year list of DVDs/BLU RAYs I've posted to my Irish Mum
A diligently collected arc of 670 film-titles, used and new
She's in her late-80s and loves to binge a good TV Series/Movie
And alphabetized, no duplication of viewing relaxayvoo

Jonathan stays and takes care of both the house and garden
Frances, Cathy and Damien call in, long-distance phone
Sandra (a Carer) drops by twice weekly to mop, do shopping
An end-of-term that's productive, family five chaperone

She's been painting art in her studio-shed for decades as well
Exhibiting and selling to a dedicated crop of enthusiasts
For as long as I can remember drawing breath, she's imbibed
Us with positivity, go-for-it credo; kids, keep up those fists

Apart from Google Duo Visual Calls to health check/chinwag
DVDs are a way for me to send out warmth from overseas
A timely film, a hard-hitting documentary, a reminder of living
Can abate loneliness, uplift with laughter and spirit please

Once she's done viewing them, they're donated to Dubliners
Recycling the recycled, they raise supplies for needy souls
She drops them into elderly friends, housebound and isolated
Locked inside during pandemic, wave into letterbox holes

I used to cycle past a pub on the Lea Bridge Road out of E17
It was renamed *The Princess Of Wales* when Diana died
I can vividly remember watching the news, so overwhelmed
Another lady caregiver, a potential-candle, lit up inside

So I keep an eye out in charity hospices/secondhand shelves
For titles I know she'll like, will fuel-fill the emotional suck
I keep the flow coming for my aging Mum who battled for us
With stories of insight, love; travellers with grit and pluck...

For my MUM, MAUREEN BARRY-WOLFE and her Carers

VISIGOTHS AT THE GATES
(Delightful Little Fuckers)

I'm holidaying in Dublin and a young Mum is delighted by her daughter
Four years of age and sun-bright as a sixpence newly minted
Hop-skipping the footpath, she breathlessly asks question after question
Holding pretty Mummy's hand; gorgeous potential unstinted

But when the teenage years turn her into an emo brooding interrigator
She'll be cringing at parents she once hugged and approved
Every word out of your mouth is delusional, biased, born of decrepitude
Would be better for humanity if you were summarily removed

Your shameful pronoun ignorance, politico incorrectness, cod liberalism
Will infuriate and embarrass them like an untoward fart in a lift
Their incredulity will morph into hints, a skull cap electrodes realignment
Perhaps consider sterilization of your genitalia a gene pool gift

Vetted opinions, audited factoids and woke gender-bender knowledge
Your young adults will expect of you a Full Metal Jacket spread
If you're not on the conscience ball every minute every hour every day
You're clearly Satan, Adolf Hitler or just plain unwell in the head

Raising eyebrows in disbelief as you explain the ways of a cryptic world
They sit patiently as if dealing with the elderly on placation drugs
Your deranged mind is like a cesspool to their superior clued-up noggin
An old computer infested with hippy-psychotic viruses and bugs

Where do our opinionated get their argumentative rage and fury from
Was it that Philip Larkin poem about all parents fucking you up?
They're suspicious of your every dodgy thought process and utterance
Poison chalice of tainted morals, *you* took one too many a sup

Or is their passionate argument fired by a bleak future we've bequeted
Are they riling at parents who cowered from Gaia's clarion call?
Or the horrible trauma of absenteeism, soul craving for real-world care
Lingering wounds from ice-cold deniers who weren't there at all

We were just as manic at that age and probably a drag shit-ton worse
Lashing out at the old world order when idiot factor was shown
You can only hope that maturity/wisdom will replace inflxible absolutes
When they have hot to trot nippers; loudmouthers of their own

In 410 AD, *Alaric I* was the only Visigoth Ruler in eight centuries of siege
To breach the Roman Empire and sack its symbolic capitol seat
But being a Christian, he urged his armies not to defile Rome's legacy
Even show old heretics some respect; curb their doctrine's bleat

Philip Larkin's 1971 poem *This Be The Verse* is revered as a masterpiece
Surmising that parents pass on mistakes, creating monsters anew
But the notoriously dismissive librarian never knew the gift of kids himself
And his cynicism is a lot like copout philosophy that just isn't true

You wouldn't wish hurt to finagle itself on any precarious sibling journey
But maybe they should dial down on their *Visigoths at the Gates*
Parents have dragged ammunition boxes and battled hate detractors
They not trying to fuck you up or deny; they're the best of mates

So don't get so sniffy my darling buds of May or any other daffy month
When dear old Mum and Dad quote from life experience gained
Because if there's one thing Philip Larkin was bang on the mulah about
It's that one day kids; *your cack report card will be similarly stained...*

For our Children's Children's Chilren
And all the Crazy Parents who bore them

WEDDING DRESS IN THE RUBBLE

Former teacher, sustainable clothing seller and now field paramedic
Anya Seledkova met trucking company owner and spearfishing specialist
Sasha Khaustov as she tended to the wounded on the Eastern Front
Four months after the Putin-led Russian invasion of Ukraine
On the 24th of February 2022...

During a shell bombardment a month after they'd met
Sasha said "I Love You" to Anya
Shielding her body with his as she nursed a soldier
Who had had his arm ripped off
They plan to marry after the war and raise chickens
And have a humungous family...

Oncology Nurse Nastya Gracheva (36) and Dentist Anton Solokov (39)
Hold two bullet casings between their thumbs and index fingers
For camera - similar to the 3mm fragment of rocket casing
That had embedded itself in Anton's left knee during a Russian
Grad Rocket attack on a medical provisions supply depot
Where he had been queuing outside on the pavement
She waiting in a nearby car with the engine running...

In immediate nursing-mode
Nastya applied a tourniquet to his bleeding-out wound
And then drove him through explosions to the only functioning hospital
In the city, where doctors temporarily saved his leg only for it to go black
From no blood supply and need further specific surgery
Provided for free by a sympathetic clinic in Munich...

Jewellery businesswoman Yevhenia Emerald is now a Sniper
For the Safari regiment and her extraordinary good looks
Caught the attention of gunner Zhenya Stypaniuk
Who met her off a train with a huge bunch of hard-to-attain flowers
And more than a lump in his throat

And not wishing to postpone such dual surety any longer
(Because tomorrow might never come)
Yevhenia was given away weeks later by a General in Zaporizihia Base
With makeshift tee-shirts and jerry-can barbeques
And with special dispensation is now in her home in Kyiv
Awaiting their baby daughter...

Police Officers Anastasia and Roman Romaschenko had been secretly
Holding hands on patrol and by invasion day were already engaged
But had been casually putting nuptials on the long-finger...

However, when alone in a city bunker filled with 100 scared young cadets
And as many officers children
And with only one gun and 28 bullets to defend all hunkered there
Anastasia began to panic and called her beau
Who talked her through the fear
And on his arrival, the crazy redhead (as she was dubbed by other crews)
Married him immediately...

In April 2022, one month before a war fragment
Had almost cost Anton his leg and life
Nastya has slummed together a leather jacket and a lace headpiece
Made from two old dresses and used sheets
Capped in place by a branch crown of entwined local flowers

And sat on his bovver-booted lap, limbs intact, both bald-headed soldiers
In the city of Kharkiv, the second biggest population centre in the Ukraine
Married under the torn concrete and steel of a home
With its ceiling missing
Camera crew (at their request) capturing the moment
To raise funds and awareness of those fighting in the war effort
For freedom from someone else's tyranny...

"Together in fire and in water..." the young Nastya quotes

Tugging proudly on her makeshift Wedding Dress
Amidst the rubble
Their combined love will one day rebuild...

YOSEMITE KEROSENE

Water-dropping helicopters along with 300-firefighters
Began tackling a raging wildfire in Yosemite Park
A giant mature sequoia is one of nature's tallest trees
Vulnerable to Nevada winds and Kerosene spark

There's a trunk amongst them called The Grizzly Giant
Estimated to be a staggering 3000-years of age
But it could be laid to waste by climate change amok
Aided by mankind's carelessness, centre stage

The nearby village of Wawona was evacuated of 600
Smoke and flame threatening, noxious nearby
But the campers cried for other reasons than blur eyes
All that nurturing beauty replaced, toxicity sky

They'll undoubtedly find the wanker and his cigarette
The lazy tourist disrespecting wondrous green
And when they do, I've asked for legacy punishment
Walk in the ashes of children; futures unseen...

For ENVIRONMENTALISTS Past, Present and Future

FEEDING SEAGULLS

In the cycle of ostracised isolated addiction and personalised Hell
I meet you with two bicycle-stolen beaten-up black eyes
But am I a naïve sucker to intervene, speak with damaged goods
Like feeding seagulls whose shrill screeches never demise

I could see it in your crest-fallen face flicking through paperbacks
Sat on your basement flat porch in the blistering July sun
I've been ignoring you and your hoodie crew of tin-holding grunts
Pissed every morning, shouting bile and cunt at everyone

Neighbours discuss getting rid of you and this constant replaying
That you unleash as you approach smiling, bumming coin
Talk of beating up your Mum in her Clarendon Road safe house
Spitting out racist bile like some footie thug kicking groin

But I saw that cornered child in your shivering morning-sober gait
Sitting there, telling me you don't give a fuck, when you do
I went to bed miserable, thinking about your inevitable social fate
Moved on again, a punch too far, a cold prison cell for you

I thought of our helpless 30-year old Autistic son cared for by many
What would happen to him if his parents didn't carry the fight?
Brutalized by a world where he's not a human being but a statistic
Another scavenger, raising bin-lids in the dead of winter night

I've determined to mention my 12-years-recovered friend in Dublin
Maybe get you into a program, keep the demons at bay
And not forever be a lonely aching soul on a counsel housing step
Maybe escape that inner screech; live life in a better way...

MAJOR, EXTRA STRENGTH

"You'd better sit down. This is going to be a shock..."

I remember my neighbour's face when she told me
And how she was just a little too pleased
To be the bearer of such extraordinarily sad news
Her horror amped up even more by my brutal and truthful reply
"At least he won't suffer anymore..."

Niall Humphries used to smoke Major cigarettes (Made in Ireland)
Extra Strength filters darker than the sedate norm of Carrolls No. 1
Few could stomach their proper-smoker lung-hurting denseness
Their suck-you-in addictiveness, in fact, a little like Niall's need

We had no terminology then for compulsive obsessive behaviour
No labels like Autism, Higher Functioning or Asperger Syndrome
No support or back up for what we just used to call odd

And indeed we did make odd 21-year-old bedfellows, the two of us
When you'd come in and we'd play albums and shoot menial shit
Maybe you sensed a kindred spirit in me, who lived nearby, went to
Stupid school together, where the pick-on persecution first began

You hadn't taken your life at home 6 January 1980 because of illness
But because of loneliness, no end to it, uncontrollable driven behaviour
And I have always regretted my own gutless refusal-to-hang excuses
On days I hadn't the strength or character within to cope with you...

So I remember sitting there, thinking God had answered my prayers.
Relieved, because I knew you were no longer calling to my front door
To get away from bullies chasing you up Castilla Park from Belgrove
Bringing you into 31 until they got bored and moved on to other kicks

It's been over 40 years and you're still in my prayers; still Dublin visiting
Grave No. 6 in Section C of St. Fintan's Cemetery, Sutton; forgiveness

Hoping to meet you one day in that peaceful place of no judgement
Where we'll never again have to reach for extra strength to survive...

For NIALL HUMPHRIES of 131 Vernon Avenue, Clontarf, Dublin 3
Died 6 January 1980 aged 21, buried 9 January 1980 in Section C
Grave No. 6 (St. Brassic section) in St. Fintan's Cemetery, Sutton, Dublin

HERCULES BOMBER

When you're young, you think your home is an aircraft hanger
And the small road you live on, a runway for Hercules Bombers

You're sure your ten-year-old besties are lifers
They've even got nicknames, shared gangly limbs, swap cards
And every football ever kicked on your hometown street
Will not become lost in the brambles lurking out ahead...

But, when you return as an adult, there are too many parked cars
The endless school summer holidays and kitchen soirees - gone
Your chums have buggered off, moved away, emigrated, died
And your once huge Mum and Dad are now so much smaller
Alarmingly frail, whisperers, when once, there was a roar...

Adult me is at a local restaurant table and majorly splashing out
Like a big boy should, like the expected conquering hero ought to
Drawn back to Dublin by the long reach of familial, the lure of home

And wallowing in the best company (working chef out of sight)
My brothers and sisters laugh along with our Mum and Dad
Competing in the stories told, sweet repartee and reminisce
Middle-aged wistful at the almost blinding clarity of times just past...

Not fixating now on how every course ever presented
At life's banquet always seemed to cost us too much
And again and again and again, as if needing to
Reaching for one more witty memory that will make them smile
Because you must make them smile, you must finally show them
You must make them know how much you value what they gave
Throughout all those decades of sacrifice...

And that come the final lift off, the last payback moment
Their grown-up paddle holders will be squat on that wide runway
Signalling the all clear, smiling, guiding the unwieldy hulk home

All the way to the horizon of another feast
Freshly laid out on beautiful white linen
By another chef who has always cooked for the sheer love of it

And smiling at his table bustle, never once considers gratuities
Only the rapture of the meal, the flight that lies ahead...

MALADROIT and ENNUI

Discombobulated with sculptural bamboozlement
Are popular reactions to a loaded ingénue
Perpendicular salutes and her elevated meritorious
Both warranted honourable mentions too

Most mullioned by your asymmetrical curvaceous
Our ennui is quite ceremonially exhilarated
Rhapsodic rods stood bolt upright and substantial
With the earth's gravitational pull negated

A fully committed aphrodisiacal red-blooded rush
Immediately invalidated any limp maladroit
As I ogled your dual proportional representations
Copping drilling rights I must urgently exploit

Libidinous and metamorphic, I needed a lie down
To mellow my overexcited centrifugal force
Any further sightings of your Rubenesque numerics
Could spark another tissue-paper discourse

Olden fugacious words don't do your zaftig justice
Head-turning babe of galactic proportions
I celebrate your effect on us, you fantastic sexpot
Inflaming our male dirigible into contortions

Long may your modus vivendi continue to enthral
And the Goddess of Venus De Milo animate
But please remember when you don that strapless
It may cause our male need to perambulate...

TWELVE-BAR HEROES

I picture you talking classic twelve-bar riffage to your musical heroes
The Howlin' Wolf and Muddy, excited like the Blues was new
I remember us discussing vinyl-albums we bought back in 69 and 70
Slavering over songs like each was *The Elixir of Godlike Blue*

I don't picture you hulked in your home unable to catch your breath
Because the second round of Stage 4 Chemo was too much
I don't think about our phonecall only days ago when you emerged
From a diagnosis and treatment kicking your body into touch

I think instead of laughter we shared at dinners in respective homes
Bad jokes about politicians, sexual prowess, old Jewish couples
Appreciating NHS-gifted second-chances in life, the miracle of kids
And how if you had your health, then, you had no real troubles

I think about your historical academia, those savvy online viewpoints
Digging deep into the Jewish experience and its ongoing story
Attending rallies and Anti-Semitic gatherings to counter the monster
Determined to bring us all back to the horror they called glory

I think of you and devoted Marilyn mock-jabbing, us belly-laughing
Joining in the jokes about piles, operations & bladder control
Remembering our parents and friends, legendary Tele programmes
And those beautiful vinyl 45s with label bags and spindle hole

So, on this sad day, I imagine you grinning at an R 'n' B Torch Singer
Grooving at the back of a gig, joint go-jumping, intimate club
Saving up memories for parties yet to come, for when we get there
Re-sharing the stuff of life, a six-schillings perforated ticket stub...

On the shock news and horrible loss of our friend MICHAEL ABRAMOV
Who died suddenly Saturday, 14 August 2021
From complications due to Stage-4 Lung Cancer
For his wife Marilyn, Their Kids and Family
Keep on rocking in the free world good friend

FIRST COLD OF WINTER
(At Your Own Risk)

Sometimes life is vicious and cruel, like a thousand lonely knife wounds
Constantly scabbing at what you've lost and will loose again tomorrow
Our son's ingrained Autism, fears for his future, who will protect our boy
Who will have his back? Be his life-support pal, when he needs one?

Other days are filled with empathy and hope and smart phone photos
You proudly display on Facebook so good friends and family can see
Spirit-lift moments that come out of left field and reaffirm your belief
In humanity, bolster up the hurt management you have to daily wrestle

Dean and I are in Margate's only running Hydrotherapy Pool & Gym
A special-needs facility the council hasn't yet axed to cut cash corners
Blue Wave session between four and five on an empty October Friday
The first cold of winter beginning to make itself known outside...

Welcoming bathwater hot, the floor jets are off and the whole pool
Is eerily devoid of sound, the big blub entirely ours to glug and enjoy
Just his beam and my pasty body wading around blue slurp ripples
Dean so totally immersed - noisy boy just loving it – gigglesome as he
Scythes the silence with open palms and excited blurt shouts...

You enter at your own chlorine risk, be aware of the needs of others
Say laminated pool rules littering the tile-walls in spaced commands
No-No cartoon diagrams; no running, no bombing and no pushing in
No responsibility ever taken, an even 1.2 meters depth throughout
Lowering cranes for paraplegics and sensory soft-tone lighting...

Like an unwieldy suitcase post abandoned ship, I'm carrying Dino
A lanky 27-year old young man in the arms of a 60-year old Dad
His face is lit up as he floats – loving the sensation and my effort
But the local kids start arriving for the 5pm Victoria Road session
So we exit to beat the intrusive bodies and their unpredictability

In a cubicle near us, I hear a proud Mum speak to her 4-year old
Her daughter with more cognitive cohesion than our grown up
"Do you need anything else besides your cosy Chloe?"
"No thanks Mum" she answers pertly. "OK sweetie..."

Juggling goggles, towels and shampoo, Mum is thinking on her feet
"Would you like them to turn on the jets love, have all those bubbles?"
"Yes please!" she says excitedly. But then falls silent, Dean's barks
As I towel him down eliciting hushed and measured explanation
Mummy asking her little girl to understand and be understanding
"It's O.K. Mum..." she replies

I wring out the two soaking wet trunks in a wall-framed hallway dryer
Its steel cage rattling and vibrating as you press down hard on the lid
Dean centres himself down by the push-in doors to the pool, then walks
Quickly, striding forward to the next bit, routines that help him navigate

Pointing his finger through the glass, I get the one-word commands
Sat with a Chunky Kit Kat and a 7-UP tin in the vending machine foyer
Just as the sound of local children screaming with laughter and joy
Permeates through the doors to us parents, quietly handling rituals

As we walk home with swinging pool bags, his peaked cap on wet hair
Dean is animated, looking forward to an afternoon of Go Thunderbirds
Me, another holiday outing filled with good stuff and a break for Mum

And I think of that natural four-year old girl and her beautiful sensitivity
Waving at Dean as she held her Mum's hand going into the pool

She must have picked up his special needs vibe in the cubicles, turned
And made sure, even at four, to single him out for acknowledgement

No pointed fingers or awkward stares
No running, no bombing, no pushing in

Just soothing bathwater on a good day

With the first cold of winter
Neither outside nor in...

KISSING ASHTRAYS

Philip Brightling was the one boy who refused to smoke
No matter the taunt; we were mightily impressed
He seemed able to resist Seventies capitulating culture
The *drinking* and *smoking* that all men caressed

Girls were gaga too for his suave demeanour/willpower
They'd shout from bus-stop seats and corner walls
Plus the fact that when they kissed, wasn't a bar ashtray
Crammed with squish butts and disinfectant balls

I tried roll-your-owns and even a pearl-inlaid Daddy pipe
In my efforts to be Secret Agent *James Bond* hip
But I could never get *Rizla Papers* to pack tobacco right
And the piddly little things kept sticking to my lip

One day at home I felt a tightening, left side of the chest
When I'd seen a BBC1 documentary, the day prior
Age 16, I immediately quit cigarettes and its companions
Scared witless by a sponge-lung-prognosis, so dire

But mostly I remember cool Phil pulling all those sexy girls
In their smocks and patch jeans, cheesecloth shirts
And thereafter, I didn't sweat lads trying to 007 emulate
Then later on clutching muscle, where it *really hurts*...

MUCH TRUCK

I've never held much truck with fancy words
Like cuckold, artifice or comestibles
I'm more a fast-food adjective kind of chap
Like a-hole or dickhead or testicles

Can't be assed with addenda, élan, prolix
Aegis, circumlocutory or turgescent
Most likely to hang with ne'er-do-well verbs
Like knob-gobbling twatty peasant

Not really partial to dropsical or supercilious
Minerva, Permian, Omanis or Xeroxes
Peter Pecker boning an Anaconda Wanda
Is way more likely to tick all the boxes

Give me a good old gobshite ninnyhammer
A proper Muppet that isn't woke or rote
I like 'em dirty and all wordage challenged
As real and as bent as a nine-bob note

You can stick your gauche, alod and nabob
Ennui, axiom and oeuvre – they all suck
Because if it doesn't have sexy street smarts
Then I don't give a double-asterisk fuck...

FULL MONTY ON THE PALISADES
(A Life Unguarded Moment)

She's always suspicious if I talk to any other women
Even if they're not the least bit interested in me
All topics are off-limits to my privacy conscious lady
Better to be in each other's thrall, no company

But I'm Irish, and so genetically programmed to talk
Chat is second nature to my curious orientation
I'll engage with the masses or just-arrived singletons
Give them the skinny on Kent's seaside situation

What she doesn't get is that, I'm still so proud of her
Shedding dress, bra and knickers - into the Sea
Mooning Half Monty on concrete slipway Palisades
Navigating the grey ripple, all childlike and free

I talked to the tanned Belgian with a Peroni bottle
And the Faversham insurer with tinted glasses
Both loving the just-right waters of a July afternoon
Free to be yourself, no judgements or passes

A handsome young couple visiting our brownstone
Now describe Margate as a *magical place*
And when I see my gal embracing such impromptu
Life hoots; high-fiving her unguarded chase...

For our MARY ANN

SHIFTY TUCO and the BULLETBELT BABES

We adored Pistolero Banditos and hot Bulletbelt Babes
Filling our Seventies teles, home from boring school
Linda Cristal, the Latino ranch wife to Big John Cannon
In TV's *High Chaparral,* made Irish buckaroos drool

Lee Merriweather played Ann in Allen's *The Time Tunnel*
Julie Newmar wowed in *Catwoman*'s clingy leather
Alexandra Bastedo in *The Champions, Avengers* Emma
On to Glynis Barber as *Dempsey*'s 85 pulse upsetter

Raquel Welch in *One Million Years BC/Fantastic Voyage*
Ursula Andress bikini-exiting the sea in Bond's *Dr. No*
Anita Ekberg in the *La Dolce Vita* fountain, Sophia Loren
Wearing anything, always had our loins good to go

Angela Sarafyan, Thandie Newton & Evan Rachel Wood
Provide the same in *Westworld*'s harsh fantasyland
Where Cowboys and Indians cannot wait to walk naked
Give those paying customers a realistic robot hand

As the executioner reads out his long list of transgressions
Tuco looks shifty on a gallows, rope around his neck
Juan Ramirez (former known as The Rat) is *The Ugly One*
A Mexican brigand working a scam, soon to collect

Clint Eastwood plays Blondie, accurate with a Winchester
Chews half-lit cigar stumps; he badly needs a shave
While Lee Van Cleef plays Angel Eyes, a merciless *Baddie*
Looking for Bill Carson's $200,000 loot hid in a grave

But these Spaghetti Men are fodder once the ladies show
Loaded duds guaranteed to make all shooters bolster
Sharon Stone, Lucy Liu, Megan Fox and Salma Hayek's bits
Haunting every young cowboy's trigger-happy holster...

WIDE BLOWS OUR BANNER
(Hope Is Waking)

With his one good eye, Malcolm stamps our English Heritage Cards
And directs us to the steps of an outbuilding housing an exhibition

Suffragettes working in the then all-male domain of gardening
Chief among them the beautiful face of Lady Constance Lytton
A key activist, imprisoned four times for public and civil disobedience

Her militant hunger strikes were broken only by trauma force-feeds
Leaving her paralyzed for life; now an ethereal photograph on a wall
Surrounded by roses and grass, nature healing the horror in her head...

Sauntering too slowly for them, dotty old English types trundle past us
Saying things with absolute posh sincerity like, *"Oh, I'm terribly sorry..."*
Their well-thumbed National Trust Guides gripped like bibles or elixir
As they giddily overtake us to catch the 3:30 tour around Vita's study

Like a Thirties time warp that obstinately refuses to modernize or update
Sissinghurst Castle and its inspirational Gardens is the kind of British hoot
That makes you want to throw up both hands into the clean woody air
And burst into a Noel Coward song, shouting skyward about mad dogs

And flighty Englishmen frolicking in the midday sun with shirtless chaps
While what-ho earnest linen ladies model indescribably racy jodhpurs
Staring longingly at the swan-like necks of other terribly nice British girls
Sweating amidst plant rows; gripping long hard handles and thrusting...

Clutching wicker-baskets with a thermos and sporting sensible shoes
Patrons chuckle as they beat you to the last few tickets for expert Bob
Who tells us stories about goers called Gertrude, Beatrice and Violetta
Breezily regaling their husband's many gay scandals in open marriages
Nibbling on cheese sandwiches as we find out who did whom and why

The stringy spines of ancient books catch your eyes and open nostrils
The charred inglenook with a history that goes back a full four centuries
Kings and Prime Ministers and Science Fiction writers all sat in this room
Puffing pipes whilst literally deciding on the fate of the Western World...

In the boudoir upstairs, impossibly tiny window-squares overlook acres
Whilst the bedside cabinet is estimated by the BBC to be 1000 years old
The cavernous fireplace and brass bedpans still reeking of naughtiness
Harold and V procreating for the tedious necessity of line continuity
Their post-romp reading tipple, "*Pot Pourri For The Southern Garden*"...

But it's the plucky feminine vibe of the entire estate that moves you
Vita Sackville West's quiet flower arranging revolution, instilling balance
Doing men's work and doing it well, nettle clumps faced, mucking in

And back amongst the wall displays of the exhibition outbuilding
I stand pride-chest hurting, gawking at period black and whites of
Pioneer groups, gathered by a naked and elegant nymph statue
Posing for posterity with such staggering grit and internal flame

Emerging from the shackles of the old, girls getting their lilywhites dirty
The Women's Land Army, the Social and Political Union, Suffrage
Ladies in corduroy, triangular-pattern tweeds and veiled sun hats
Staring at the picture-taker with a barely-contained ferocity...

And on the wall beside them is a reproduction page to a 1911 song
Reciting the lyrics to "The March Of Women" by Ethel Smyth

Her words of freedom thundering in the silence
In this refuge for stoical souls, this place of woman-power
Grappling hook the change that must be fought for
With white-knuckle bravery...and bare hands...

"*...Shout, shout, up with your song!*
Cry with the wind for the dawn is breaking
March, march; swing you along
Wide blows our banner and hope is waking..."

For every SUFFRAGETTE everywhere

INSPIRED CHOICES

I remember my secret thrill as you grooved in your evening hairnet
To the fabulous Blues Rock of TEXAS and their fantastically alive
1989 Debut album "Southside" on Mercury Records with the sexy
Sharleen Spiteri on Vocals sided by Ally McErlaine's blistering axe
Even your ungainly air-guitar moves, so cool, and yet unknowing...

I'd ache as you laughed with other men who didn't really get you
Saw this young pretty peach as just another notch on a long boast belt
And I'd sit on a high stool in Fleeming Road and smile along to stories of
Growing up with savvy Yiddish kids in Stoke Newington, heading home
From school with pal-joyful Joyce who protected you from bullies
Storming Grodzinski's of Stamford Hill for kosher bagels still oven hot

I'd listen to love songs on the CD Walkman; pacing E17 streets at night
Trying to figure out my place in a world post divorce
A sad refugee from a failed marriage that started out so lovingly
But ended up so sectarian cliché

And then when I did move in and that magical tie-die night happened
I looked out the next morning through the back garden window
At a slice of mowed grass that suddenly seemed beautiful and ordered
Rather than ragged and forlorn

And that afternoon in Eileen Daly's house when you turned up with a *blue*
And we both wept at news that was hardly unexpected
But still (both of us at 33) mind-blowing and life-changing

Then trekking across London in the snow to work in a Mail-Order Music Co.
An hour and a half each way; every day; four trains
And although never expecting it, I'd come home to a cooked meal
And your fab blond hair and round face and growing loveliness

And all the while knowing deep down inside why I'd held out for so long
Why I'd travelled through slush and mist and so much drift
Why I'd arrive at my new home, at our new life
Thanking the great celestial riff-making machine in the sky
For *inspired choices*...

For MARY ANN, Her Friends and Our Journey

SLITHERING IN MY ROOTS
(Rinsing Mr. Deflated)

Weary after another successful sortie into someone's psyche
Mr. Deflated checked into The Double Negative Hotel
He showered quickly - then exfoliated any pallor and residues
Of dead dreams, broken hearts and such like bagatelle

Took a motivational video by Professor We're So Hard Done By
Grateful for seven highly effective whinging techniques
Had breakfast with his mentor Capt. Let's All Obfuscate Today
Ordered up assassination attempts on 6 positivity freaks

His favourite Eighties band is Frankie Goes Absolutely Nowhere
And their seminal debut Welcome To The Poo Poo Dome
His preferred haunts are sweatboxes, latrines and a McDonalds
He'd buy a prison, but there's a tax on a second home

Mr. D. enjoyed the incarceration flick The Fuck All Redemption
As a tunnel of shit almost asphyxiates Andy DuFresne
But he intensely disliked the upbeat ending about a new start
And there needed to be far more no hopers in frame

Mr. Deflated has signed up to a lifetime membership for sloth
At his nightclub That Chip On Your Shoulder Really Suits
But I for one am considering getting me a professional haircut
Rinse out his despondent colours a-slithering in my roots...

BREAKDOWN IN CUSTODIAL SERVICES
(Dear Oh Dear)

The Wonder of Men – Part 1

I recently sent my wife back to the sanatorium as a matter of urgency
And not because of defective ironing or independent thought
She began to engage in all manner of worrisome personal enjoyment
Like eating meat, reading, fresh air; I was nauseous, distraught!!
(Dear Oh Dear)

The administration of *Doolally House* sent me a diatribe on her account
Claiming I must be having a delusional male dominating laugh
But I said this was outrageous slander, why only last week I extended a
Tungsten chain from her kitchen sink by a good foot and a half
(Dear Oh Dear)

You can trust my fiscal impartiality blossom, I assured her most assuredly
So I'm off to the Genting Casino, Wetherspoons and the Bookies
I'll be having deep conversational exchanges with the Latvian Barmaid
Who only wants me to fully appreciate her EU self-raising cookies
(Dear Oh Dear)

I've told my wife the Catholic Church has generously agreed to forgive
Women's distasteful call for equality with 1 million acts of contrition
Because only last week, we saw a woman exit the Upper Deck of a bus
The outrage? She hadn't asked the male conductor's permission!!
(Dear Oh Dear)

Be with us in our hour of need Great White Protestant God of Manliness
As we allow women freedom to go beyond Persil, Ajax and Vim
In the meantime I see my wife on the front porch with a large secateurs
Must want to clip some irritancy, give her vegetable patch a trim...
(Dear Oh Dear)

UNCLE MOXIE IN THE CHEAP SEATS

The first time I asked for a drink was in a Co. Waterford boozer
On a school-holiday with my family, I'd sneaked away
I walked up to the 1970 bar and ordered a pint of Smithwicks
Pointed to its lit-up red neon logo, my uber casual play

But I went puce as I blurted out my best older-man impression
A moxie boyo having attended grizzly elocution classes
Underage or not, he didn't miss a beat, countered his towels
Began pulling that froth into one of his cleanest glasses

In the same backwater town was the crappiest cinema ever
Actually had wooden benches, rock hard budget seats
They were showing the 60ts Bond-knock-off *Man from UNCLE*
With a bad projector that missed crucial dialogue beats

After my successful alcohol duping, I sat glued & resplendent
Ireland's very own all-conquering corduroy Duke of Earl
As I watched Napoleon Solo and Illya Kuryakin outwit THRUSH
Save the world, look so cool, AND get the gorgeous girl

But of all my recollections of that fateful day, pondered most
I've always asked myself, why did he serve me that sup?
Although I came far too close in my teens and early twenties
Drinking's easy evil never did settle in as I finally grew up

Memories are deceptive buggers, screening out horror paths
Where life could have slipped into an addiction drown
So when I think of laughs, I counter them with a cold comfort
As I see his varicose face back-pulling that lever down...

WE LAUGH AT IT NOW

I once chased my younger sister Frances up the stairs
With a kitchen knife, as brothers are want to do
We'd had a teenybopper kerfuffle about Rock Songs
So she had to be terminated by you know who

Though it seemed like perfectly reasonable behaviour
At the time (an appropriate harmless response)
She took umbrage to my serrated blade-jab offensive
And called me a phrase not dissimilar to nonce

Three decades later, reminiscing as sibling grown-ups
We recalled other antics cutting a memory rug
And realised that what was once so damn important
Has become a future punchline, derisive shrug

We laugh at it now of course; even admire its passion
And children testify that Fran did indeed survive
Today I look with huge brotherly affection at my sisters
And thank blunt cutlery, that we're all still alive...

For FRANCES and CATHY

ROMEO REMOVAL PILL
(Where's Elon When You Need Him)

Relationship rejection inflicted on us in our teenager years
Returns in our dotage with undiminished power
When our heartache felt like a tornado-malicious sinkhole
Just hearing a love song could all hope devour

Adventurous youth populate TV Shows and hipster movies
Flitting from one loved-up wall-slam to another
The elasticated-heart dime-dropping undying devotionals
On the head of the latest more fanciable lover

Is it that our race has been run and our love number is up?
As we smile warm at other people's happiness
The years melting into wrinkles and routines and tablet vials
And bedrooms with little to celebrate/confess

The mistakes we made in love all those vivacious eons ago
Creep up on us in our unguarded moments still
So I keep watching pretty young things living their best lives
As I wait for Elon to invent a Romeo-removal pill...

SCHTOOPING MR. NICE
(Judgement Day Committee)

I want to fuck the pencil pusher in a Ralph Lauren knock-off
Is not what top totty in city offices long to share
I cannot wait to have my bum pinched by an old manager
Pick nits out of a yawning computer nerd's hair

Sipping contemplative wine, women brood in discreet snugs
It's time to lose exciting types and put down roots
They're looking for someone to share a cavernous IKEA with
Paint white picket fences & knit wee woolly boots

Their days of ordering hard-on lingerie from buff catalogues
And adjusting car seats, is long a thing of the past
Looking to settle down with a suburbanite in pressed slacks
Who won't leave aging relatives agog nor aghast

To date there's been a succession of truly beautiful women
Arriving down from London at our seaside Air B & B
Towing with them men clearly punching above their weight
Not exactly Tarzan or Einstein with sizzling repartee

They've traded in Johnny Handsome and his winklepickers
For someone they wouldn't have looked at twice
Settled for polishing Mr. Dependable and his sensible shoes
A malleable schedule for Dry-Schtooping Mr. Nice

We're all playing an ongoing game, self-tweaking our parts
But should we be content with a calorie-empty pie
Stood in front of a disconsolate *Judgement Day Committee*
As they turn our *lived* pages, shake heads, and *sigh*...

PENNY ON THE WHEEL

We were talking to our neighbours Bob and Angie about tricks
Our parents used to do when they were a little broke
You'd prize open the Bakelite cover of the Gas Meter junction
Put a penny on the wheel, slow it down; con the yoke

Young mums would borrow a bowl of sugar, baking soda lump
A couple of eggs, a whisk and a wee slaver of butter
You'd dodge the rent-man bullet, hire purchase payment due
By relying on the trenches, generosity to one another

Jan and Rosa spotted us when the readies were most needed
Our Jewish pal Gloria painted us portraits for naught
Ted and Jared mucked in with vine pruning strangulated trees
A crew of ladies work our gardens, no longer fraught

Joe D, Morelia, Rachel, Freidar, Sophie, Nico, Joanna and Raz
The Craigen Family, Lisa and Aidan, due recompense
They've all helped our helpless Dino over the challenged years
With patience beyond pounds, schillings and pence

It's astonishing how lonely/isolated overcrowded cities can be
And maybe we need to get back to the ways of old
When a chinwag with a neighbour, or unexpected generosity
Would be all your reading needs - stave off the cold...

For our NEIGHBOURS and FRIENDS of the FAMLY
Who've helped us out over the years, as we have helped them

LONG FALL TO FREE

In September 2001, seven days after the Twin Towers in New York
A 38-year old British mother and her 11-year old Autistic son
Also leapt, feeling they had no choice, no more options, jumped out
But away from horror flames of a different kind

Unable to cope and unable to bear her son being taken into care
Helen and Mark Rogan walked onto the Hownsgill Viaduct
In Consett, Co. Durham and jumped 180-feet to their deaths below...

Beneath the five inverted arches of Gill Bridge (as it's known locally)
Are trees and shrubs grown tall and strong since its 1858 opening
As an old world line designed by hero engineer Robert Stephenson
So, side-by-side, in deep foliage, a brother-in-law found their bodies
Notes to family and friends, addressed, waiting back in their home

Devoted to her boy and with father absent, she'd left work in 1996
To dedicate her life to his raising, but the difficulty wore her down daily
So I think of the day we lost our boy Dean in Walthamstow's Lloyds Park
When he simply got away from us and was gone for more than five
Minutes of agonising and praying; those pleas answered as he turned
Up back in the place where he'd left, back of his own Autistic accord

But the memory of that split second took-your-eye-off-the-ball beat
Has haunted us for decades since – the moment we almost lost him
Horrible, like that afternoon we had to acknowledge our growing age
And leave him to live in a special needs community in Stonehouse
Gloucestershire, us sat in the car park bawling, his bewildered face

We know Helen Rogan's Purgatory, nerves shredded by moods
Fatigue days, the cold decisions that rip you up inside
When nothing is fair in love or war or on ancient viaduct
Where walkers can enjoy the view of nature in all its splendour
Watched by an absent God, opening his hands
Only to catch ashes he should have looked after better
Feeling the reality of a calculating system
Unopposed vulnerability laid-out in the distance
Where his younger beauty will no longer protect him
Feeling the unlocked abandoned car that will never be returned too
As two desperate souls hold hands, left only with the long fall to free...

For HELEN and MARK ROGAN

YOU DON'T HAVE TO BE MAD TO WORK HERE

Preserving the past became a sort of thing for us in *Reckless*
Self-confessed vinyl junkies, foldout gatefold in hand
Buying and selling albums and singles and rob-wallet rarities
The must-have music from your chosen artist or band

I'd kerfuffle in front of Terry O'Sullivan's *Loricraft Audio PRC 6*
A hand-built professional record-cleaning machine
Listen to the thread play the music while it sucked up gunge
Revitalising the grooves of another curvy evergreen

We'd open at ten, close at seven, the sounds never stopped
Cram a shuffle-play with every possible genre need
The jokes would fly around as you served the religious faithful
Double-check grades, artwork, label's up to speed

You'd still get a thrill from those 60ts and 70ts laminate sleeves
Genuflecting in front of legends, assuming position
But as the decades marched on, what was once so plentiful
Became so difficult to get in a playable condition

After 20-years of buying and selling huge collections of worth
I swung a heart-attack at 54 and never did recover
I've still got the RR Neon from the window of 30 Berwick Street
The shop that's featured on the Oasis *Story* LP cover

But my fondest memories are of me with the boys and the gals
Shooting the spit about albums that really mattered
And the thrill of finding that rarity you'd been lusting after yonks
Before we lost Peel and our teenage kicks shattered

Too many of our musical heroes are now shedding mortal coils
And it's a process that sadly goes on now, unabated
So I crank up the amp, lift up the Perspex lid, talcum on the lino
And *Get Back* to *What's Going On*, my *Soul* elevated...

For all the STAFF and CUSTOMERS bought from and sold to
At *RECKLESS RECORDS* in London's ISLINGTON and SOHO

PARADISE PRONOUNED
(Cancel Culture)

The Catholic Church has been forced to refurbish Purgatory
Due to an unprecedented influx of Venial Sin
The overseeing committee for Shitheads and Semi-Fuckwits
Decides who gets excluded and who gets in

Lucifer, however, is arguing parameters for greed and vice
And is unhappy at their pronoun interpretations
He maintains that in order to be a proper cunt in UK politics
You should copy Nicola Sturgeon's inclinations

She leads the way in stabbing your former allies in the back
Then claiming you had no idea what was lost?
Flagellating Scottish Independence to death with bullwhips
Whilst secretly pissing your kilt at the fiscal cost

God has managed to remain a non-inclusive independent
And refuses to be drawn on such piddly things
It seems his gift of freewill to mankind continues to bugger
As we sabotage any Utopia the future brings

So maybe I won't listen to Talk Radio or surf a poisonous Net
Where society's know-it-all twats seem to lurk
Looking for some new angle to hang the *Cancel Culture* on
While the rest of us rise early and haul to work

Like radicalized Muslims, so many cults dictate sideways bile
As they battle it out for the jurisdiction of Souls
I long for a future where Gilead is named as freedom-ruinous
Just another book of male dominated controls

Paradise Pronouned/Segregated isn't anybody's truth, ever
Include instead, all of God's diverse creations
Because the more I witness how overlording enables haters
The more I'll crave, a life free of manipulations...

SOMEONE'S CHILD (Lucia Te Amo)

There's a lady from Surrey in her 80s
Paddling by the Margate Sea edge in the blistering sunshine
Thoroughly enjoying the cool water
In her sensible linen blouse and long floral skirt

It's a beautiful Wednesday in late August 2022
And young again, invigorated, she smiles as she passes
So clear she says, terribly pleased that it is
As if only to confirm the hunch she had
To come down on a coach day-trip to the Seaside
And recharge the batteries...

There are three sets of parents with their be-hatted toddlers
Also on the clean sand, also then venturing to the edge
Splashing and giggling in the near ripple-less wash
Catching the spread of outgoing tide that is free of seaweed
Yuck that would tangle around feet and scare the young ones...

On Monday of this week, two days ago, a 9-year old girl
Was shot dead by a callous masked gunman
Chasing a 35 year-old burglar into a random Dovecot home
Bubbly Olivia Pratt-Korbel dying later of her chest injuries
In a Liverpool hospital Emergency Unit
Her Mum wounded too as she tried to keep harm out
Devastated staff, inconsolable parents, family numb, lost...

On the seawall by the Margate Lido, some holidaying Italian kids
Have taken nearby clumps of the abundant white-cliffs chalk
And carved out love messages on the concrete path below
Thoughts that are unaware of pain
Lucia Te Amo, *Isabella Te Amo* (I Love Lucia, I Love Isabella)

I see them in my mind's eye on further days out at the seaside
Splashes, refreshments, playing, sandcastles under a friendly sun
Looking back at the love on Mummy and Daddy's face, reassured

And not a second's thought given to where the monsters lurk
In the cold random expanse past the safety of the shore...

For OLIVIA PRATT-KORBEL and her Family

YOUNG AGAIN

I know it's a cliché to soft-focus your long-gone sophomore past
Like it was a golden age, all uncomplicated and shiny new
And yet from a journey distance of over fifty-years, I'm still there
So many of those transcendent moments, still echoing true

I think about old fleapit cinemas and the myriad movies I ogled
The thrill of a good fantasy flick or a killer comedy writ large
Someone's multi-layered story of tears, a triumph over the odds
With the tie-in credits song making mush-punters cc charge

I've always felt young just sitting there, checking out trailers first
My candy stash at the ready as the curtains swished again
And I wasn't so dumb as to not know I was being manipulated
By experts in emotional juicing, pulling triggers of joy & pain

But why do great old movies linger with us, written on our hearts
Visual vignettes of life made by arty others daring to express
Because they're reflections of a love and belonging we pine for
A way out of all that too-too-real stupefying single loneliness

Nowadays the graphic gore shots pour out of uber-realistic TVs
Fast-edited, gaudy-worded, throwaway women splattered
But I long for those old romantics when I actually felt something
When holding a girl's matinee hand, was all that mattered...

THE LONG HAUL
(Light In The Shadows)

Simon in Bed 19 suffered a massive heart attack at work
A marathon runner and physically fit
Even in the longest steel bed frame, he's tall-building huge

Simon Austin is 32; not the usual patient in Ward 3E
Of The Royal London Hospital in Whitechapel - Stroke Section

Lying still, his cranium is stapled
They removed half his skull to relieve the pressure

It's a long haul now for his young wife and family
Feeding him yoghurts, working towards mash

But when visiting hours are over and that uplift filters away
They still leave their talisman, their light in the shadows

Beside a small circular shirt button that says *Best Dad*
There's a large colour photograph
Cellotaped to the trolley at the end of Simon's bed

It's a picture of his two beautiful children
Giggling on a beach in the sand
Lifeforce coursing through their veins...

I look at it too, and know why it's there
In Bed 20, in my angina pain
I look at it too, and well up

You focus on your children; you focus on the love

And like Simon's Family, you think about the long haul
You muscle down hard; dig in for the long haul, find the light
And you keep on going...

For SIMON AUSTIN and His Family
For James Walsh and Mybarik Zaiui (The other two patients there)
And Nurse Sinead O'Connell who helped us all
Stroke Section, 2 to 4 Nov 2012 at The Royal London Hospital

SUGAR LUMPS ON THE COUNTER

At Reckless Records in Upper Street, Islington, and Soho's Berwick St
In my capacity as chief knowledgeable type for vinyl rarities (20 years)
I began getting contacted by BBC types eager to shed collections
A lifetime's worth of now surplus platters (most unplayed)...

It started with Jeff Griffin walking into our Islington cellar and *liking me*

Producer at Live Aid in 1985 and Engineer on so many BBC sessions
Jeff had a thing for the Irish, and trusted me

But the swine denied me his trio of Nick Drake Island Records originals
Grinning as he fanned them in front of my lusty eyes (no go boyo)
Then Jeff's staggering collection led to something even bigger
John Walters, John Peel's Radio 1 Producer from 1969 to 1991...

John was the kind of wit and English gent who lit up a BBC microphone
And blessed with impeccable taste and uncanny suss
For decades, Walters was Peely's ears on the ground

Always up for a lark, a visiting Beeb crew set up for a gag-based show
So we did a sketch of us manically chasing down an original 7" single
A withdrawn A&M copy of the £10,000 Sex Pistols *God Save The Queen*
Where John stood in a phonebox calling up dubious dealer types
Me keeping nicks on the outside for dodgy Vivienne Westwood ruffians

Another skit between his LP racks, John gassing to the cameraman
About sound (year 2000), "This Mark Barry! He knows his stuff!
He says CDs are like having the band in your living room!
(Looks to the camera alarmed) Do I want *The Troggs* in _my living room_!"

I was three days at his Oxted home packing 168 boxes, four-tiers high
(5-days valuing John Peel's collection too, when he passed in 2004)

But mostly, I vividly recall a pub conversation we had during breaks
John sat there (misty-eyed) telling me about this friend of his
Who'd come running into the control room in his first year with J.P.
Raving about a singer he'd seen in a London bar the night previous
A *Folk Lady*, his 1969 pal enthused, with the voice of an angel
It was of course *Sandy Denny* of Fairport Convention and Fotheringay
And the only vocalist invited to duet with Led Zeppelin ("IV" in 1971)

Ever scouting artists for Peel and his radio show, Walters went along
And said the hairs stood up on the back of his neck when she sang
But then suddenly blurted out, "Oops! I'm going..."
And raced to the bar (who knew him and his needs) for sugar lumps
Put there in a bowl to stave off his Diabetes blackout and possible fall...

He returned giggling, crisis averted...

But I don't remember the relief, just laughs in his kitchen, tea bags
Biscuits dunked, a full run of Peel Sessions 12-inches kept
Memories too good to be parted with
Helen talking of her time managing The Bee Gees at their peak
She asking after our Autistic son Dean with genuine concern
When I least expected it (still does all these years later when I call)...

But mostly
I can still see John's face of awe in that bar as we sat there talking
About Sandy Denny, The Alan Price Set, Georgie Fame, Ray Charles
The Beatles, Dr. Feelgood, The Specials, The Fall and The Cure...
And his widow's smile (Helen) as she saw our connection over music
Her mad husband in his element with a similarly moved journeyman

It was the same at Bernie Andrew's funeral
He showed me the toilet roll John Lennon had nicked from the loo
Property of the BBC typed on every Izal sheet (tickled him pink that)
Standing at John Peel's graveside with the lyrics to The Undertones
The same *Teenage Kicks* he'd framed in his study
Sheila scooping her bubbly 2-year old grandson as if he was sunshine...

A member of their audience giving these heroes the nod
Tearful at sugar lumps on the counter of life

Remembering with such affection
These people vessels of something deeply beautiful...

For the Broadcasters, Producers and Pioneers at the BBC
JEFF GRIFFIN, BERNIE ANDREWS, JOHN WALTERS and JOHN PEEL
And All Their Families

DECLAN and NEVO SAVOUR THE SUNSET

Mount Melleray is a Trappist Abbey in Cappoquin, Co. Waterford
We'd holiday there as a family for two weeks every July
Snuggled into the Knockmealdown Mountains since its 1833 build
It's all spires, incense & padded pews under an Irish sky

The gardens surrounding it stretch up the thicket in each direction
Tamed by Christian Brothers in practical self-sufficiency
They grew every foodstuff they needed to live and kept bee hives
Homemade bread, churn butter, strawberry jam for tea

Father Nevard and Brother Declan were the ones we'd hang with
A spiritual, Nevo was kind, generous with all that was his
Declan was a Cork Man with a fiery temper and a searching mind
Could fix anything, mechanical repairman doing the biz

In later years my younger brother Jonathan struck up a friendship
I can see him and Declan tending to the vegetable rills
Laughing about life, politics, slugs, cack decisions and sportsmen
A mentor for my brother climbing rough relationship hills

The Brothers saw God in green fingers, welcomed with examples
And lived a life few in our modern climate would attempt
They'd maintain the old buildings through donations & produce
Try to keep sabbatical affordable even with coffers spent

No young blood embraced the austerity, constant body losses
Have done for the Abbey, survival and future under threat
But with such affection, I recall the simple credo & higher plan
Tend to the soil, help people in need, savour every sunset...

For NEVO, DECLAN and my brother JONATHAN

PACK MULE
(Clinging Sand)

Sometimes I feel like an old pack mule
Traipsing towards some unattainable better horizon
Straggling along at the tail-end of a seemingly serene Caravanserai
Overburdened, frightened and sinking

Other times, I all but inner glow as the sun comes up in the morning
I walk down the street literally smelling the roses

Like that time I was shuffling barefoot on Kent's *Joss Bay* in April
Beach solace, warm on the skin
With barely another soul in open view

No one going at me with a pock-holed well-greased blame-spatula
No one moving around arrogance-spittoons on shifting sands
Fly-whipping the tired exposed skin of age-old touch points
Like health, family and money worries

No late-life rounds from a sniper-rifle pinging past my exposed head
Emotional tank tracks to be avoided

Just walking peacefully
For miles and miles and miles
With only *smooth* up in the distance...

We all carry the baggage of living on our bent bones axis
Huffing and puffing
Hoping the long and winding road will indeed bring us back

But take us forward too
Into a less brutal place
On to a kinder set of dunes

Where even pack mules
Get a chance
To shake off the clinging sand...

BEEHIVE and BOUTONNIÈRE
(Crossing You In Style)

Jean Vera Wilson was our neighbour of some 30 years in E17
They shared 28 Penrhyn Avenue with four grown-up tots
Angela, Alan, Richard and youngest (budding writer) in Lucy
Council house, did the pools, garden of vegetable plots

Jean used to paint as a young woman in the Swinging Sixties
Sold her railing art on the Portobello Rd, groovy and hip
But married at sixteen to an older man to a Beatles backdrop
She became a stay-at-home mum, took a different trip

On her memorial booklet by The Co-Operative Funeral Care
Is a photo on the rear of a teenage curl girl; happy grin
More of a young woman marrying Carnation Buttonhole Ken
She in her Dusty Springfield beehive hair, fashionably in

Even when we moved into 30 Penrhyn Avenue in early 1991
Jean was frail from a lifetime addicted to filter-tip fags
She'd bake us hot apple pies that I swear stank of cigarettes
Always thoughtful, thankful, but her eyes, sunken bags

There's another fab 60ts memory photo of a chic suited-lady
About town in her Audrey Hepburn *Moon River* beguile
And that's how I think of her with a dapper boutonnière Ken
As they both relive glam lives, crossing that river in style…

For JEAN VERA WILSON, 5 March 1948 to 12 July 2022
Our Neighbour and Friend in Walthamstow, E17, London
Her husband KEN and Family too

NORTH AMERICAN EAGLES

I don't see you in the scruff or in the torn metal
Or in that scorched pilot-suit you were born to rock
Nor do I see you in the distant dust cloud and smoke plumes
Or in that tiny square hard-drive that miraculously survived
To tell your astonishing legacy

I see you smiling at camera, talking spit about thrust, honouring
Your hero stunt lady and land-speed record holder Kitty O'Neil
A deaf woman with no limits in 1976, balls to the wall courageous

I see you lighting up at the sound of motorbikes and car engines
A team of men who look at you in awe, who care beyond words

I see you addressing the impudent boon and its endless questions
About why a girl would choose lunacy and danger and uncertainty
Over home and kids and stability

I see your whoop and high-five devotees when it all goes right
The feeling of being alive, achieving awesome despite externals
The fearless attempt after attempt after attempt
Those gorgeous baby blues twinkling at the lens
In your thirties, but coming on like a teen given the keys to Nirvana
A kick-ass rodeo gal who came good, telling youngsters to dream

And then, test runs over, with a tip of Ed's keepsake baseball cap
You give a nod to those you love (and who have loved you back)
Grinning in your precision machine like a sonic boom Amelia Earhart

And cockpit calm, I see you thumbs-up the tech team once more
Then visor down, push that svelte bullet past a six-mile long 540 MPH
Leaving us all in the dust as you become legend and inspiration
The cool tomboy in her custom-built *North American Eagle* Jet Car

No, I don't see sorrow or regret, but your fabulous unflinching spirit
Rising up to the embrace of those who've gone before
Earthbound families below, waving at their brave rocket girl
Finally free to soar in that great record-breaker gig in the sky
So few will ever have the nuts to know...

For JESSI COMBS and KITTY O'NEIL - The Fastest Ladies On Earth

ROUND and SKINNY BOTTOMS
(Reasons To Be Cheerful, Part 4)

We're on a beach with too many bikinis that don't fit
Blubbery flesh bobbing out of tummies and buns
Lager tins and beer bottles glisten in the July sunshine
Complimenting tattoos of skulls, skeletons & guns

We all claim to be diligently watching our poundage
As we quaff down doggies of convenience junk
But the truth is, we're the generation of obesity twats
Pretending that any figure is gorgeous, sexy hunk

I'm one to talk/cast aspersions with my bulging waist
And free fall torso, I find depressing to mirror see
More round than skinny bottoms, shadowing our kids
Not the best way to be future-there for progeny

There's way too many lard-asses cardiac-avoidable
Too many of us citing irresistible outside forces
So as I sit in the Spoons avoiding fries and Pepsi Max
My *Reasons To Be Cheerful Part 4*, <u>less</u> courses...

187

SHARP INHALE

I was a goner in Mrs. Dunwoody's Bed and Breakfast
As you dressed for our first Dublin night out
My gorgeous English gal correlating duds of appeal
With a splash of swivel hip and lipstick pout

But it wasn't 'til we entered Harry Byrnes bygone bar
As a snug full of men and Guinness set sail
That I knew I'd struck gold in a shaped velvet onesie
Loins prepped, ticker gone, a sharp inhale...

ON THE NEXT GO ROUND

We drive past Balgriffin Hall where Mum and Dad first met in 1957
Into Fingal Cemetery on the windswept outskirts of Co. Dublin
We make our sibling pilgrimage along the immaculate rills/rows
Jets paying no mind to loss, as they continually roar overhead

Dad is laid to rest just a few feet away from a Naughty Fallen Traveller
With the most cluttered OTT-garish Liberace-proud burial plot
A mad marble shrine, Guinness pint glasses and boxing memorabilia
Winning Belts, Teddies, Photos and even a bench for the weary

You'd have appreciated the one-upmanship of final best-plot dibs
And laugh at the social irony of the company you're finally keeping
But in our culturally enlightened 2020's, not everyone is best pleased
Adults rendered child-raw by a gaping hole deeper than six feet...

Our Poppy of 86, who spent his whole life guiding nervous patients
Through crippling and lonely paths of self-debilitation and grip fear
Is within eyeshot of some thirtysomething slipshod yahoo and ruffian
Who forfeited his far-too-young life in a bravado brawl gone south
And of course, there's the inevitable bull of family squabbles
Signs of our post-loss memory-ownership on lavish engraved plaques

But it's three years on, and I suspect you're no longer fretful or worried
Instead, you turn your bright eyes to the grave immediately right
Where two broken-hearted parents buried a stillborn baby girl there
Who we're also told, were so overwhelmed with grief; couldn't return
So now, without a remembrance stone or border, her spot is sunken
Our derided travellers showing hero-heart, bouquets freshly placed...

I suspect you love us still Dad, and intercede when our needs must
But today you're laughing and shaking hands with the goer boxer
Whose showing you how quickly his hubris-knuckles mended
Trying to catch his wild accent and truly breathy lust for life

Smiling too, at a three year-old, as she picks meadow-flowers
Excitedly explaining her exhaustive plans to run through fields
Gathering up nature's love and the sweet caress of healing

And how she's going to spread it all over lots of sad people
And family, and even strangers too, when she's all grown up
And on her next go-round...

SHARKSKIN WEAVE
(Old Order Got To Go)

Things were simpler in the past and lawlessness an urban myth
Is the mantra of every TV/Net philosopher, hip and astute
It was all double-breasted Sharkskin Suits, gent-tipping Fedoras
Neighborly living in the ascendance, no trickster or brute

Perhaps it may have seemed that way on the buffed porches
Of white picket-fenced suburban palaces of moral clean
But legal banishment to asylums for unladylike insubordination
Was the reality of the undertow, *institutionalized* obscene

Women had no real say in the rose-tinted view of pearly-white
The viciousness of male laws hidden beneath fisted greys
Today you're encouraged to turn on yourself on palm laptops
Dance to puppeteers; sign up to vitriol and smug malaise

War, genocide, torture holds, walls to keep out dirty immigrants
Is the appalling track record of a corporate-bought *male*
Men may talk it up when it comes to embracing a better world
But give them power or office and *inaction* is their prevail

Be wary of the race to go backwards; a snake oil compromise
Tug that chain, the more retro-obsessed media becomes
Because if you're not careful to actually secure a lady's future
Then all you'll ever have is brush-offs, tables full of crumbs

Slick Willy may come on all smiling-beguiling at campaign time
But is that wolf ever going to produce the pro-lady goods
Because all I see are so many women sleep-walking to Gilead
While Rooster smirks in his immaculately *intransigent* duds

Instead of hankering after a compromised sepia-tinted mirage
We need to run towards a future that let's everyone grow
And as much as I love you ladies, stop being a sideline gullible
Don your power-suits, force legislation; *old order got to go...*

YES NO

Yes to the short but beautiful life of Gabriel Hardisty-Miller
Hackney's *Person of the Year* 2009 – an inspiring young Autistic Man

Yes to family, friends and fighters like Beth, Graeme, Mary and Ben
Who helped him find his unique style and gave him a way to express

Yes to the NAS's *Think Differently* lobbying campaign, GM speaking out
Being interviewed by UK M.P. Phil Hope for the AUTISM ACT 2009
The first British disability-specific-law to meet the needs of special needs
To protect them, facilitate independence; safety for all the Gabriel's

No to lucrative zero-facilities privately owned care in the community
Homes that used this law to make money out of the most vulnerable
Gripping epilepsy that hit aged 7; a river raft of mood controlling drugs
His parents fought until his passing in Aug 2012 to neurological decline

Yes to the NORDOFF ROBBINS Music Therapy Centre in Lissenden Road
Yes to men with beards and newspapers that made Gabriel giggle
Yes to him being silly as he slid under tables to avoid hearing authority

Yes to the Spice Girls, House & Indie Music, Beat Poets, DJ-ing as PIGPEN
Yes to gigs, inspiring others, giving slots to Asperger's Syndrome singers
Yes to step mum and pal Mary Lemley who loved him through Autism

Yes to a simple YES/NO tap device that allowed him to communicate
Yes to his cool glasses and beautiful childlike face and wild blond hair
Yes to Music and its staggering healing power; its deep soothing waves
Yes to chords and voices and guitars and drums and bass and pianos

Yes to a young man with headphones on, laughing, walking into sound
Arms outstretched, no fear, no regret - on into the warmest welcome
A place where all expression is accessible
And different no longer matters...

For GABRIEL HARDISTY-MILLER (19 May 1987 to 4 August 2012)
MARY LEMLEY-MILLER And GRAEME MILLER (Mum and Dad)
And his Carer and Friend BEN CONNORS

PAPA BEAR EXPLAINS REGULATION LENGTH

You see this whole *having children thing* has thrown Dad for six
Because your father is no longer the centre of attention
Now there are cots and rattlers and aromatics to be changed
His Subbuteo and Scalextrix are relegated to detention

Now I know it seems that he's on many forms of lysergic drugs
Should your noise levels and demands rise above a zero
And that recent meltdown about a Rusk-encrusted TV remote
Made him look like Herr Hitler channelling Emperor Nero

But as he adjusts my dears, you will see encouraging changes
His tranquilizer dosages plummet to manageable sums
As he pushes you about on tricycles and talks to the teachers
Administers to wardrobe malfunctions, pets upset tums

By then, you may notice, that he smiles when you do stuff well
But in your teenage years, his old discretion takes a hike
As any male suitor of his daughter over hair regulation length
Can sling his licentious hook on his Flash Harry motorbike

It only gets worse as you approach adulthood and beyond
Adjust to friends, partners, rent bills and the working life
Laugh and cry and travel and explore and go much further
Than he ever did in those rearing years of chaos & strife

Your father may be potty, but he'll love you unconditionally
No matter where your heart makes landfall in the foam
What he fears and desires most is the pivotal moment when
You finally put down anchor, key into your starter home

So spare a thought for *Dear Old Dad* with his *Mumma Bear*
Both with an eye on the TV and the other on a phone
Worrying still, but always lit up when diversion is interrupted
With *contact*, leaving him feeling less parentally alone...

For FATHERS and their CHILDREN

THE NEXT STAGE (Soldiering On)

Three ladies close to me live with Stage 3 Breast Cancer
A *Wife*, *Sister* and *Aunt*, all battling the cell's caress
But what was once a death-sentence is now controlled
With Chemo and Surgery, necessary horrible duress

We men don't comprehend such real physical brutality
Until in our Fifties when habitual binges come to call
Heartbreak hoarded up in angina arteries and body fat
Blood pressure's skewiff; engine parts gone into stall

Medicine will one day tablet-defeat every horror cancer
A final neurological win that caps a life-denying war
And a hundred thousand eulogies will be reread, solemn
As survivors mark the day disease can hack no more

A woman's identity is more than body-physical attraction
Yet an attack on it feels like something gold is gone
Still they face the next stage with endurance and bearing
Wounded and maimed, head held up, *soldiering on*...

For MARY ANN SIMMONS, CATHERINE BARRY
And ROSETTA SIMMONS

CLOAKROOM MEMBERSHIP IN THE V&A

If you're a critical white man, you can *only* become a racist
My inherited class and privilege guarantees it so
And if you've a higher education, owner of a large business
You're oblivious to humanity's poverty and woe

My wife and daughter visited the V&A Museum, Kensington
But got search-stopped by the cloakroom head
Black man insisted Mary Ann's membership was out of date
Would have to huff heavy bags around instead

Our Julia had purchased a delicate dress in a *Zara* boutique
A lilac linen folded by an assistant and bagged
But Mr. Arrogance insisted on searching with deliberate digs
Only to crush it all back in, misshapen/snagged

A complaint in another office confirmed his rookie's mistake
And blush apologies were manifold and profuse
But my missus knew why he'd created such a visible shamer
When some grandee insisted on cloakroom use

Mary Ann hadn't got the right kind of distinctive enunciation
Nor sported her correspondingly old school tie
But the reverse racist practically flooded his Downton liveries
When Lady Uppercrust fluttered her gentry-eye

When I read about corruption in the USA People's Collective
Public funds siphoned off to blag another house
Is it any wonder the eradication of millennia-old race inveigle
Make the dual-aspect blame-pyre hard to douse

We've come a long way from the horrors of the *Strange Fruit*
The Aryan Race Jackboot and Nazi Stuka scream
I just wish that *all colours* could honour MLK's coexisting vision
Else it will never be more than *his beautiful dream*…

LIBERAL TERMS

Mr. Bumble whacked his winter staff on the town-flyer numericals
Showing that a mere £5 secured his parochial goods for sale
"Liberal Terms!" he fed to a Mr. Sowerberry, sceptical Undertaker
Scowling at the bother of another half-starved/deathly pale

Mr. Bumble had been offered three pounds and thirteen schillings
By the Board of Corrections, grimy chimney-sweep's employ
So 11-year-old Oliver Twist becomes a lucre workhouse profitable
Maybe later become army fodder, more innocence destroy

Children were indentured, enslaved and abused by heartless men
And the British Author riled against it with all his literary might
It's why Charles Dickens is beloved, a humanitarian to commoners
Always keeping it truthful, sickening child injustices, highlight

There are grooming gangs in Britain still, who prey on special needs
Working on the compliment, so physically unable to defend
But the real reason child abuse still exists in 22 is because authorities
Refuse to take on monsters or laws to imprison them amend

He'd seen inside debtor's prisons, known the despair of foundations
Where good society hid away people for a petty transgress
Locked into a cycle of enforced ignorance and open-ended abuse
Few ever made it out into a loving embrace, a family bless

When Oliver Twist was serialized in 1837, Dickens had chronicled evil
Few in power were prepared to admit to, let alone see reform
And in Paradise, he's still reading them fantastical adventure stories
Smiling down on their restored faces, extoling *love as the norm...*

For CHARLES DICKENS and all the early Humanitarians

EMPEROR PALPATINE'S SKIN MOISTURIZING TECHNIQUES

Emperor Palpatine's Skin Moisturizing Techniques is my favourite book
Went to Number 1 on the Health And Happiness Guru charts
Second only to *Benny Hill's Halitosis Tips For Chasing Girls Around Trees*
And that stunner, *King Kong's Repair Guide For Biplane Parts*

Proportional Dynamiting of US Mail Trains by Butch Cassidy is a blaster
I ate up *Fire Extinguisher Brands You Need To Avoid* by Jaws
Sports Bra-Fitting For Megalomaniacs with Three Nipples by ES Blofeld
Gave my undergarments regimen a definite cause to pause

And who can forget *Luke Skywalker's Guide to Surviving Daddy Issues*
Or *Cleopatra and Marc Anthony Quietly Toss Caesar's Salad*
I've dog-eared my *Travis Bickle's Successful Handbook to Taxi Driving*
Cherished my *Joker's Face-Painting Classes with Sulfuric Acid*

Removing Difficult Stains On Hand Towels by a blameless Pontius Pilate
Was also a huge smash with Jimmy Saville, working at the BBC
He read *Effective Lollipops* by Chitty Chitty Bang Bang's Child Catcher
Sent a copy to Prince Andrew, proudly pert in his Royal Library

Getting The Most Out Of Sunblock by Icarus has always been a sizzler
Is almost as good as *Finding A Faithful Wife* by Henry the VIII
But my all-time upsetter is *Panting And Panties* by leggy Sharon Stone
Liable to make my basic instinct hard and nutsack palpitate

Life would be dull without cinematic pyro-techniques/gross-out laughs
Kenneth Williams crying *Infamy!* In the brilliant *Carry On Cleo*
And huzza for *007's Best Ever Magnets For Removing Women's Zippers*
Running Up Walls In Crotch Tight Leather by The Matrix's Neo

So here's to the Chippendale's buff masterwork *The Buns of Navarone*
And the BBC's woke cooking epic - *Sex, Lies and Garlic Bread*
And *Running Up That Stranger Things Hill* with Kate's Upside Down Bush
As *Capt. Kirk's* Phaser gives his Spock, some enterprising head...

196

THE INDEFINITE FUTURE (Our Format In Hand)

The problem with maturity and growing up is the child within
Who dances still and never wants to grow up at all
The impact music has had on my life amounts to more than
A huge Rory Gallagher poster on my teenage wall

With albums under my arm, I'd strut down our 32-house street
King of the world, the oceans, the sky and beyond
James Taylor, Bill Withers, Carole King, Led Zeppelin and Joni
Beatles, Stones, Budgie, CCS – all the magic wand

As decade passed into decade, multiple genres intoxicated
Like Prog, Soul, Fusion, Blues, Folk, Reggae & Glam
Barrier smashers like Pentangle, Television and David Sylvian
Tighten Up and Philly Intl. LPs, made me who I am

You could buy albums by Kevin Ayers, Labi Siffre and Genesis
Horslips, Donny Hathaway, Marvin Gaye and Al
Later it was The Clash, Talking Heads, Prefab Sprout and Jam
Every type of musical journey was a spiritual pal

And the solo artists who impressed so deep, rationality gone
Dylan, Bowie, Elton, Springsteen, Carly and Kate
Paul Simon, John Martyn, Dan Fogelberg & Jackson Browne
Produced solace, often made heartache abate

So many of our heroes have passed into legend that it hurts
When we used to maybe sigh if 1 or 2 was taken
Prince, George Michael, Joe Strummer, Amy & Two Beatles
Elvis & Bob Marley, losses that left many forsaken

Mañana is the Spanish for tomorrow or *The Indefinite Future*
And lately, the format wars has been reversed
Vinyl is surging again in popularity; even girls are buying LPs
And they don't have to be boyfriend-coerced

Can it be explained away as just a song that touched you?
Made you want to boogie or just sit quiet in repose
All I know is that since I was 10 and held *our format in hand*
I've always loved music & Vogue still strikes a pose...

For VINYL LOVERS and SECONDHAND MUSIC STORES everywhere

CLUE ME ONE TO TWO
(Maybe Even Moved)

Outside the Sundowners Nightclub that faces Margate's beach
There's a bandstand erected to schmooze hot clientele
At a microphone is a singer loudly crucifying Jungle Book songs
Disney songwriters ordering up a gallows, hoods as well

Should I slag off this amateur-hour George Michael for his efforts
Or clap hands for his guts at facing a disinterested crowd
Because, while Louis Prima who originally sang the song, is gone
He'd have smiled at a grafter trying to do legacies proud

Every forgotten has perfectly rational reasons for not going for it
But the decades go by so fast and then you're out of time
So *Clue Me One To Two* Mowgli on man's indomitable reaching
And pour gallons of your Firestarter, on everything I rhyme

Our years on this terrain of sinkholes, elevated ridges and mirage
Is determined by gumption and chances, none approved
So sing out your strangulated renditions my blusher-eyed Sinatras
Until some punk takes notice; others, *maybe even moved...*

For all PERFORMERS and ARTISTS everywhere

HURT SHOVELS
(Digging Down, Digging Deep)

I'm wandering the legendary Sissinghurst Castle Gardens in Biddenden
Secretly hedged into the Wield of Kent's gorgeous duck-and-dive hills
An estate home to the decidedly racy bon viveur *Vita Sackville West*
And her hubby of forty-nine years, the British diplomat *Harold Nicholson*
She landscaping, he taking afternoon tea with Churchill and H.G. Wells

Bought in 1930 as a ruin and brought back across decades of devotion
The gardens reek of soil-toil and dirt-love and the scent of myriad plants

A marble statue of a barely-robed Narcissus heads up Lime Walk
Reflecting a Lesbian woman and a gay man's terribly British marriage
Of good old English dottiness up two-fingering stuffy puritanical peers
A tangible aroma of Heaven-on-Earth and free-forming open spirits
Amidst wildflowers given space to get jiggy with prig chrysanthemums

Emmeline Pankhurst and her war-battered Suffragettes stayed here
Recuperating from prison, handcuffs, beatings and force-feedings
Gardening the gore away with shovels and hoes and manure barrows
Nursery-weaning geometrical lines of gladioli, honeysuckles and roses...

Now hung on the Estate's gallery walls are all those steadfast heroines
Staring earnestly into the lens in linen shirts and huge tweed pantaloons
Home Front girls being practical, mum, making things grow out of mess
Then returning to cruelty and the cudgel, no matter the personal cost...

78 planks wind up the spiral staircase inside Vita's beloved Clock Tower
The worn wooden handrail and narrow steps, exhausting on the legs
Up, up, up to a steel gate now blocking off her writing study with 2,700
Volumes of poetry, political critique and horticultural analysis
Left just as it was when she passed in 1962, Harold in 1968...

Uncovered by restoration on the Tower walls are plaster-carved graffiti
3,000 French prisoners interned there during the seven-years war, 1763
Drawings of sailing ships, the names of sweethearts, longings for home...

And I think of *Noor Inayat Khan*, an Indian Princess who became a spy
Parachuted into France aged 29, captured at 30 by Nazis and tortured
Raped repeatedly, but gave up no comrade, naught but her name
Crying in her dungeon alone, until a friend in a nearby cell
Heard her last defiant word before the bullet - *"Liberté!"*

And in this ancient house of sanctuary, I'm reminded of continuance
Of handmade ceramic angels watching over struggle
Instilling peace into brutalised minds and war-battered limbs

I'm reminded of friendship bracelets and engraved pocket watches
Precious keepsakes and carefully bowed twine around handwritten
Letters that took effort and patience

I'm looking at those young unflinching faces as they stare back at us
Damning the begrudgers and the naysayers and the grubby monsters

Digging down, digging deep, pushing those hurt shovels into the earth
Establishing beds, displacing obstacle, taking on all-comers

Facing off against the endless tormentors and the inhospitable terrain
With unspeakable bravery...

For the SUFFRAGETTES and Sissinghurst
For my sister CATHY, and my wife and her mum MARY ANN and ROSA
All living with Cancer

BAZ AND FRANKLIN INADVERTENTLY GO BANANAS

A pasty-faced Irishman and chubby-cheeked African American
Enter the South Woodford Odeon in 2008 with no idea of what's on

In a moment of rash yet Mensa-on-the-go type decision making
They settle on a movie poo-pooed by the critics but publicly beloved
Mamma Mia – a feature film with a *lot* of ABBA songs in it
And Meryl Streep wondering whether or not she should shag
Pierce Brosnan, Colin Firth or Stellan Skarsgård, *again*...

Arriving late, we're armed with Chunky Monkey and Banana Split B&J
Twin scoops and Coke cartons bigger than Paraguay's national debt

We quickly seat ourselves just as the credits are about to roll
But the moment the dappled-sea hits the screen, it's then we notice
That almost all of the small audience is decked out in truly garish
Seventies-period *ABBA* outfits, and all the punters are *men*...

Up come the lyrics to each song with a bouncing ball across them
And the entire audience goes into mini-microphone waving routines
Mikes they brought along to accompany the spandex and frills
As they start laying into a full-throated Sound of Music Sing-A-Long
Because that's what it is - a *Sing-A-Long* showing of *Mamma Mia*...

Gobsmacked and loving the madly gay Danny La Rue hootenanny
Two different-coloured men sat in their seats, B&J ice cream mid air
Chocolate and Banana flavoured hetro types tittering at their luck...

I have many memories of Franklin like that, the two of us on the raz
Having a laugh, indulging in our dual passion for big-screen movies
And cool food acoutrements that sported way too many calories

And now he's gone, passed after years of complications from a stroke
His grown-up kids Lauren and Selase mourning his loss on Facebook...

So here's to the *Super Troopers* and the *Dancing Queens*
To when we hooted with the boys in tights through *Voulez-Vous*
To the young-at-heart and up-for-it friends, enjoying life's mess
To laughing with the best audience, going loco, going nuts
Swimming towards the sunshine umbrellas in an all-encompassing sea...

For our friend FRANKLIN KWAWU and Family

STANDING STILL, MOVING ON

On the grass in front of a spray of flowers
Arms and hands resting on up-bent knees
My Dad is smiling for the camera, seventy years young...

Eighty-six years of age hasn't happened yet
Nine years of bone-marrow cancer
The long dignified struggle with pills and hospitals
A Lancet case study for endurance against the march
Expensive stomach injections containing microbes
That will eventually get the better of him

It's a favourite photo on my iPhone
And I see it every time I take it out of sleep mode
A daily reminder of savouring life
Enjoying love and your children

But it's also a pang of pain, a red-raw wound
A half dream that's hard to grasp
Will Mary Ann and I one day grace a desktop?
A skinny flex-bendy voice-activated mobile device
Smiling for our kids before the final slog or sudden descend...

It's Easter Sunday, 12 April 2020
And the news is filled with a strange brew
Of horror and hope, life and death
The massive statistics of Coronavirus, Covid 19
Hammered home every day on TV

There are acts of kindness, human decency and bravery
Alongside staggering selfishness and pig stupidity
People acting like it's all some netherworld
Affecting *everyone else* but them
Nurses and care workers staring down the onslaught without PPE
Authority screaming stay in or die, protect the precious NHS
So they can protect you, when the siren calls...

John Francis Barry smiles out at me, at us
Left behind without masks, sat on the grass in the sunshine
Contented and already in a better head place
Ready for the storm to come, no big deal for big Daddy
Standing still, moving on...

EXPOSED TURRETS
(That We Might Live)

So much in those years was an open wound
Fifty-six consecutive nights of bombardment on London
Homes and businesses in rubble, dead bodies, limbs
Communities hiding in tubes with mugs of tea and sticky buns
Nutritional combos of Orange Juice and Cod Liver Oil
For the children in danger of rationing rickets
Whole worlds held together with gaff tape

I stand at Manston in Kent where blue plaques recall so many names
Eighty-years and counting, 1939 to 1945
The individual and collective World War II heroism
Hammering our now candy-assed response to the murderer in the East

...Those who didn't come back, those that did and lived full lives
Are also commemorated beneath trees with benches for the weary
And as you sit in the light breeze, you're filled with
Visions of young men climbing into cockpits to keep England free
The pilots and crews of so many sorties leaving all in the mess hall
With no guarantee of a safe passage home

It's full of ghosts, this strangely uplifting yet humbling place
And there's the hand of God in the details too
The gunner who survived three different squadrons
When the loss of life was huge in those exposed turrets
An entire nation helping out with the meat, butter and sugar
The British bunkered down, holding on, ignoring the shells

I'm standing at Manston and tears are rolling down my face
For those who died that we might live

And alighting on all those blades of grass by the fencing are butterflies
No longer wary of the huge vulnerable by the wooden people-tables
Now overflowing with plenty

Manston in Kent, home of the Spitfire, Hurricane and Lancaster
Where the memorials count time and remembrance-planted trees
Never stop reaching for the skies...

For PILOTS and CREWS who gave their lives so we could be free

WHERE THE LIGHT GETS IN

Most mornings, in dishevelled jammies, I'm cleaning large sash windows
Last week's newspapers and Sunday supplements my latest shammies
Purging yesterday's coagulated detritus with a nation's Brexit concerns
Newly improved *Jiff*, squirt-cleansing Donald Trump's latest twat-tweet

Avoiding headlines heralding some drug cartel's casual body barbarity
Life's ingenious and ongoing cruelty for medical conditions *nearly* fixed
Warning articles on corporate greed where all the little guys get fucked
By unassailable oligarchs money-raping their already subsistence lives...

Do I need to know about 30-years of lightweight *Good Morning Britain*
The ex-cabinet minister who vehemently denies dark-web kiddy porn
A sea of plastic choking our once mighty oceans with global asphyxia
Or how ultra-fast fibre-broadband can save us all for only £51-a-month

Avoiding thoughts of my sister's recurring cancer, Mary Ann's narrow
Escape from the same, my levitation off a bed when a heart chamber
Blew, my Dad's recent passing and my once strong Mum's vulnerability
Keeping these new-home mega portals clean, where the light gets in...

Mind glimpses of me standing in the early shower at St. Bart's Hospital
With a kindly male nurse attending, watching over the slippery danger
Clutching a wooden talisman in my palm, terrifying heart Angina, pain
Shaking with humiliation, thinking about lost loved ones and the kids...

So I wipe away tree sap, blood-red berries and pigeon dinner dribbles
Use some crumbling Euro country's own-goal out-of-control debt crisis
Tame this endless bad news, removing clogs with sensible application
Obsessing over smudges that become visible with the glare of sunlight

Keeping the portals clean, where the light gets in...

CELEBRATION DAY

I'm proud of us getting this far intact with unbroken fidelity
Surviving temptation, child heartaches, disease
None of your pocketed cheap out-of-town hotel receipts
Chanel No. 5 in the morning, Brut on the breeze

We've not riding gear sticks or slapping up bedroom walls
In a frenzy of extracurricular ripped-shirts screwing
But we still hold hands on the street and kiss watching tele
And I've got your body, whatever cancer is doing

Ours is a steady flame that sizzles low rather than torching
That works life with kindness, with love, healthy wit
So I don't care what others may surmise behind our backs
We're alive this Valentine's day; ain't that the shit...

SIGNIFICANT OTHERS
INDEX of POEM TITLES and SUBJECT MATTERS
(ALPHABETICAL ORDER)

INDEX cont'd...

INDEX cont'd...

INDEX cont'd...

INDEX cont'd...

INDEX cont'd...

INDEX cont'd...

INDEX cont'd...

INDEX cont'd...

INDEX cont'd...

Printed in Great Britain
by Amazon